To: Wendy

May this book inspire "The Princess" in you!

Lisa Jones

Don't Mess
With the Princess!

Lisa Jimenez, M.Ed

Published by
Rx Success, Inc.
4630 N. University Drive
Suite #449
Coral Springs, FL 33067
(954) 755-3670
(800) 489-7391
www.Rx-Success.com

ISBN: 0-9705807-5-4

Manufactured in the United States
10 9 8 7 6 5 4 3 2

Editor: Vicki McCown

Dedication

This book is dedicated to my daughter Auriana, a princess with boundless love and unlimited possibility!

I still remember the day your dad and I sat in that doctor's office excited about being pregnant with you yet scared to receive shocking news...

"The sonogram shows a small hole in the baby's spine," the doctor informed Mark and me as we sat in his office stunned with the words. "We have to do more tests." He concluded.

After several weeks of countless doctor visits, we were told it was possible that you, our first born baby would be born with spinal bifida.

We didn't even know what spinal bifida was! But both your dad and I knew we wanted you no matter what. So when the option of aborting the pregnancy was presented to us, we denied it and carried you full term.

And on August 14th, 1989 you were born with a healthy spine and a miraculous healing. And that's been your life ever since!

You are a powerful force on this planet Auriana. I love watching your life because it's an example of Princess Power and a life that works.

You and your belief in 'anything is possible' caused your dad and me to create a loving and supportive friendship through divorce. That's a healer! Thank you Princess Auriana, for seeing the royalty in every person you meet and for being the example of feminine power.

You are the inspiration for the "Don't Mess With the Princess!" message. Thank you for claiming your feminine power and being the Princess who makes an incredible contribution to the planet!

I Love You,
Mom

Table of Contents

Acknowledgements

To My Three Children:

Auriana, I dedicate this book to you, my Princess of Possibility!

Beau: I love your dedication and sense of commitment. Whether you are at school, drawing, playing soccer, guitar or a video game, you give it all you've got! I also love your ability to balance things with your great sense of humor. Thank you for teaching me to see the lighter side to life!

Connor: Thank you for teaching me the power of kindness and generosity. You have such a gift with people. I love walking the halls with you at school and watching you greet every person you see by name. That is amazing!

Mark Jimenez:

You are the best former husband ever! I am so grateful for our friendship and that we get along so well even through divorce. Thank you for being the wonderful father to our children.

My Dad and Mom:

You taught me to value myself and my femininity from the first days of my life. Thank you for your commitment to raising children who honor themselves and others.

My siblings:

Renee, Chuck, and Scott: You helped me become the woman I am. Thank you for your love and support.

Peter Schlosser:

You are Fun and Freedom! I wouldn't be able to write the Princess message without you. You believed in me and this project before I did. Thank you for holding me to such a high standard. You are a Real Prince and I thank you for always treating me like a Princess. I love whooshing around the world with you!

Linda Richichi:

Thank you for your loyalty to me as a married woman, going through divorce, and as a single woman. Your love for me healed me through the toughest time of my life. And your commitment to our friendship is what a true Princess is all about.

To My Starbucks Friends:

John, Mona, Stacy, Randy, John and Ken. For a world traveler, it's so wonderful to walk into the coffee shop every morning and see your faces and know there's a seat waiting for me! Thank you for your friendship.

Randy Gage:

You were the one who came up with this project idea. And you were the one who first saw the "Princess" in me. Thank you for always taking a stand for me and bringing out my greatness.

Donna Sandberg:

You are an inspiration to me as I watch you run multi-million dollar businesses in your most powerful way ~ your femininity. You are a Princess of the boardroom and in life. Thank you for your example and your friendship.

Todd Isberner:

Thank You for enlightening me to what my name means, "Consecrated to God". Your prayers for me and this project gave me a supernatural power.

"The future belongs to those

who believe in the beauty of

their dreams."

—Eleanor Roosevelt

Airplane Pilots
and Airhead Periphery

I sat down in my first class seat on Delta Airlines just as the pilot's voice piped in over the intercom: "Welcome to Delta Airlines. We'll be taking off shortly for Boston and should arrive on time..."

Now, before I finish the story, I want to ask you, as you were reading that first paragraph, whose voice did you hear as the airline pilot? Did you hear a man's voice or a woman's? Hmmmm... That's very revealing as to where our culture's mindset still is—and where your mindset is too! Shifting that belief is exactly why I wrote this book!

Now back to the story...

The *female* pilot finished her announcement with a cordial, "So, sit back and enjoy the flight." Almost immediately I heard a woman in front of me lean over to the man sitting next to her and say, "Oh shit, I get nervous when it's a woman pilot. Flying a commercial plane is a man's job!"

I sat there, stunned. To think that comment would be made by a female, a businesswoman flying first class in the year 2006, was shocking! But she said it—and in doing so declared to every person on that plane and to the invisible, subconscious "ear of the universe" that women don't belong in leadership positions!

My dear reader, may such a statement NEVER come from you or

me. Please watch yourself and the beliefs—especially the subconscious beliefs—you hold about women. These negative comments keep limiting beliefs alive.

So what about you?

Do you celebrate your female colleagues or feel jealous of their success? Do you acknowledge a woman's promotion or complain about how she didn't really deserve it? Do you rejoice in the engagement of a friend or secretly hope the relationship doesn't work out because you're envious?

Make no mistake about what I am saying here. Women must get over their jealousy, limiting beliefs, and gossiping habits before they can usher in transformation. And, most importantly, women must understand the power they hold in their words, thoughts, and beliefs of other women! The point is...

You have the power to transform the world by the thoughts and beliefs you hold, the words you speak, and the space you create for women's success!

If you really understand the power you have, then you will stop gossiping and start inspiring! You will put an end to envy and begin elevating! You will kill off your cattiness and initiate celebrating women's success in business, relationships, and in life.

Will you make a promise with me right now that you will be the type of woman who celebrates the success of other women? If you just made that promise, please e-mail me at Lisa@ilovetheprincess.com and share your decision with me.

What would the planet look like if every woman reading this book made that commitment and stuck to it? Wow! I see a world where even more women are working side by side with men to discover cures for diseases. I see a world where more women are working side by side with men to protect our rights and freedoms. I see a world where even more women are partnering with men to promote peace and unity in our political field. Do you see it too?

You have the power to transform the world by the thoughts and beliefs you hold, the words you speak, and the space you create for women's success!

And that's what this book is all about...

Don't Mess With the Princess! is your guide to break through self-limiting beliefs and reclaim the most abundant and powerful force on the planet—Femininity!

There is an overwhelming call in our world for women to step up, celebrate their femininity, claim their power, and be the healing force they are meant to be.

Is that woman you?

If so, congratulations! You are joining me and millions of other women in a transformation. Women have been given an opportunity that will create a transformation for themselves and the world.

From the boardroom to the bedroom, when you embrace who you were designed to be as a woman, you will create the most successful and profitable business, attract loving relationships, enjoy a sense of peace within yourself, and give balance and harmony to the planet.

My goal is that, after reading my book, you will be empowered to: **Reclaim Your Femininity, Humbly Receive Your Powerful Purpose, and Go Out and Kick Some Ass!**

All my admiration,
Lisa Jimenez
35,000 feet above the earth on my way to New York City!
Seat 2B on Delta Airlines

"When nothing is sure,

everything is possible."

—Margaret Drabble

Chapter 1
The Queen. The Duchess. And The Princess.

Inside every woman lives three people: A Queen. A Duchess. And a Princess.

These three "ways of being" have helped you succeed and survive in your life. Yet, if we take a closer look, we would realize two of these "ways of being" actually keep you from a more successful and fulfilling life.

The Queen is overly dominant and bossy. In business, the Queen thinks she has to act like a man to succeed. In relationships, the Queen is excessively controlling and assumes she has to force or manipulate others to get what she wants. In life, the Queen secretly believes everyone is out to get her and so she has to constantly be on guard.

The Queen is exhausted from running every person and every situation. She is often alone. And most of the time, in the end, the Queen is beheaded!

Most women were taught we had to fight for our rights. We had to fight for:

The right to vote.
The right to be heard.
The right to entrepreneurialism.
The right to control our own bodies.

I am grateful to the women who paved the way of equality for you and me. However, somewhere along the way the women's fight for rights got out of balance. We have pushed the pendulum too far and today we have women in leadership, relationship, marriage, and life whose habitual reaction when faced with controversy is to jump into being the Queen or the Duchess.

It's not about burning bras, denouncing our femininity, and seeing men as the enemy. I don't believe smart women ever stood for that extremity. My Princess message is about celebrating your feminine power and partnering with men and other women as *One Human Race* to get on with healing the ailments of the planet!

You, as a Princess, have the power to put an end to "It's a man's world" and create "It's a human being's world" through your thoughts and beliefs about what being a woman is really about.

Inside every woman lives three people: A Queen. A Duchess. And a Princess.

The Duchess sees herself as second place. In business, the Duchess thinks others deserve the promotion. In relationships, the Duchess thinks her needs and desires are not as important as others. She's the one who takes the burnt piece of toast because she wants to be "noble." In life, the Duchess continues to attract situations and circumstances that keep her small. The Duchess lives a life of quiet desperation, knowing there is something bigger inside her screaming to get out!

The Duchess lives her life in fear. She plays small to fit in. She hides behind her husband, her children, and her faith. She uses submission to never step out and make a difference for the world.

The Queen and the Duchess come from the ego. They are protective energies that are rooted in fear. The temptation to play these two roles comes from the fact that they work—or at least they seem to. For centuries women got what they wanted through maneuvering and manipulating, controlling and coercing, submitting and surrendering.

But at what price?

We have to ask ourselves, "In the end, when we get the love, the power, the leadership, or the feeling of being noble, is it worth it? And, most importantly, is it real?"

You will begin to "Make a Difference" and create a major contribution to the planet, when you stop:

- Holding on to limiting beliefs, thoughts, and habits;
- Blaming men, society, culture, or religion for your state in life;
- Apologizing for your talents, power, and success;
- Acting small to fit in: and
- Denying your femininity!

Inside every woman lives three people: A Queen. A Duchess. And a Princess.

The Princess celebrates her femininity and is fiercely committed to protecting it. She responds to life's challenge instead of reacting to them. She attracts what she wants instead of forcing and coercing. She knows how to manage instead of manipulate.

In business, she surrounds herself with a great team that balances her weaknesses and complements her talents. In relationships, she knows her value and attracts people who are respectful of her and of her desire for a healthy relationship. If she chooses to date or marry, she brings out the Prince in her man and together they create an abundant Kingdom.

In life, the Princess sees herself and others as royalty. And so, she handles challenge with confidence and grace (and a healthy sense of humor!). She is fiercely committed to her purpose and, no matter what anyone says or thinks, she gives herself permission to live that purpose out loud and in color! She holds on to herself, not giving too much of her energy away to her Prince, her career, or her children.

The Princess is Feminine. Fierce. Demure. Daring...

Inside every woman is a Princess!

And the most important aspect of a Princess is her femininity. It is femininity—which the Chinese culture defined millennia ago as "Yin" energy—in every woman that brings balance in our world.

The Princess Brings Balance

When women embrace their Princess Power (the Yin energy) they bring a much needed balance to our world.

Yin and Yang represents one of the oldest philosophical theories in life. The theory has continually astounded simply by its fundamental truth about the nature of our universe.

The yin/yang symbol is a metaphor for the constant dance between the masculine and feminine energies. **Yin** is the female energy, the intuitive, receptive, nurturing side of ourselves. Yin is the energy that yields to the forces around it, flowing, and smooth—a force that allows a seed to germinate in winter and makes water flows smoothly around a stone in the creek. **Yang** is the masculine energy—the strong, action-oriented, forceful side of ourselves that gets things accomplished. Yang is the force that makes a seed sprout in the spring and makes strong flowing water move or sculpt the stones in a creek.

Let me give you an example of the Yin and Yang Theory in a modern context.

Anyone who is familiar with computer language knows that all computer programs are written in binary code. There are only two symbols, 0 and 1. So no matter how complicated a program, it can still be broken into codes of 0 and 1. This is a good example to show how simple components can be interwoven to create things of enormous complexity.

Speaking at a larger level, we can say that everything we know about in this universe is either matter or energy or a combination of both. In life, everything has opposite sides—Yin and Yang. If matter is Yin, energy is Yang. Similarly if earth is Yin, sky is Yang. The same goes for the sun and moon, day and night, man and woman. They are all Yin/Yang kismet pairs and one cannot be without the other.

In terms of energy and matter, energy can't exist without matter, and matter can't exist unless it has energy to keep its structure.

Does that make sense?

Think of it this way: Next time you listen to a song, realize that the notes being played need the silence in between each note. Without the silence the notes would not be a song. Without night we would not have day. Without dark we would not have light. Without Yin we do not have Yang. And so it is with the balance of energy.

Without the Princess, we would not have a Prince.

Are you beginning to see the power you have with your femininity? I smile when I write this because I realize how much God loves His people through His design of creating man and creating woman.

Woman. Man. Yin. Yang.

It is the most beautiful balance of energy in existence! Just think of what our world would look like is we realized the power of this balanced energy!

It would look like beauty. It would feel like peace. It would sound like harmony. It would be full, whole, and complete.

Now, you may be thinking, "Why are you writing a book for women when men also need to shift their beliefs about being a real man?"

Yes, a shift in beliefs is needed by men, too. However, I truly believe that in matters like this, where a healing and a recreation is needed, women are the stronger sex. We just are. We're wired that way. We are natural creators and healers. And women, when they embrace their femininity, will be the driving force behind this transformation.

Do you still find yourself thinking "Why me"? Get over it!

We women have such a vital mission that whining about our role will keep us small. Creating new beliefs and new paradigm shifts will greatly benefit you and everyone in your sphere of influence. Focus on that and let's get on with the incredible privilege of ushering in balance, healing, and transformation.

The Princess is a powerful force. And inside every woman is a Princess. What keeps the Princess small, shy, and silent? It's the voice of limitation and the limiting beliefs it represents. Let's talk about how to silence the voice of limitation in order to discover, celebrate, and unleash the Princess in you!

Silence the Voice of Limitation

Let's do something fun... Let's talk about your weaknesses!

Which of your qualities do you want to improve? What areas of your personality you would like to work on? Try this exercise. Set a stopwatch or timer to sixty seconds, then in the space below, list as many of your weaknesses you can think of.

Ready? Go!

List of Weaknesses:

_____

_____

_____

Okay, great! Did you write for the entire sixty seconds? Notice how well you know your weaknesses. You can rattle them off like you've been studying them for years!

Now, let's do the same thing with your strengths. Again, set the timer for sixty seconds, then list all those things you're good at—skills, talents, personality traits, etc.

Ready? Go!

List of Strengths:

_____

_____

_____

Great! Wasn't it interesting how much harder it was to list your strengths? Every time I do this exercise in one of my programs, I am shocked at how well people know their weaknesses and how difficult it is for them to tout their strengths. THIS IS A DISASTER! If you cannot boldly and powerfully list your strengths, how are you going to have the posture you need to attract the opportunities and people you need to create your Big Dream? You are up to Big Things! Playing small does not serve you or the people around you. You know this intellectually, so why hasn't it sunk in?

It's understandable why most people are challenged when it comes to stating (and living) their strengths. Culturally, this is not how we were raised. Think of it. As a kid, you were most likely told not to brag about your straight A's, your first place award in your school Olympics, or the winning home run you hit in the bottom of the ninth. Why is that? It's the "lack" mentality again! Within our culture, the belief that there is just not enough good stuff to go around is rampant. Our culture runs on the mentality that if one person wins, then somebody has to lose. There is always a winner and a loser. So we grow up with the innate belief that if we are successful at something, that means others were not. In other words: *If you are successful at your career, then your success is causing others to fail!*

Isn't this ludicrous?! But that is the internal belief that is running our lives and keeping us small.

The women who are most successful in the business world and in the dating world are the women who know who they are, respect their worth, and celebrate it!

Breakthrough Your Belief of Lack and the 'I'm Not Good Enough' Belief

It was my first year as a professional speaker. Thrilled to have found a career that lit me up so much, I loved connecting with the audience and positively impacting people's lives. And I was good at it! Or so I thought—until the first time I shared the stage with other speakers.

I had been invited to speak at a huge business convention, scheduled to speak second one evening. As I sat listening to the first speaker, I realized how good she was. As her speech went on, I revised my rating from "good" to "great." She had the audience laughing with her, and she related with them on a level that created tremendous impact. As she continued, I first became nervous, then anxious, and finally completely panicked—so much so that I had to leave the ballroom, the victim of a crippling anxiety attack. I hurried to the bathroom, looked in the mirror, and told myself that I just didn't have what it took to be a speaker and my message what not that important.

HA! WHAT A CROCK!

What I want you to notice first about this story is I created my own anxiety! Please don't miss that point. I chose to listen to the voice of doubt and limitation. And, here's the really important point: It wasn't the voice of limitation that caused me to have an anxiety attack. It was my choice to listen and give in to that voice that caused my acute anxiety.

Why in the world would I let myself create such personal panic? It's because the principle lack and limitation is alive and well in our world. It prevails because our culture does not believe in abundance (yet)! The unconscious belief of limitation explains what happened to me in this way:

If the speaker going on before me was good, then she used up all the "good" and there would be none left for me.

Do you hear how ridiculous that is? It's like saying there is only a certain amount of love on the planet. So if Leslie gets love, then Lyn doesn't. Or, there is a limited supply of health on earth. If Danny is healthy, then Sara can't be.

But what's the reality in life? *We live in a world of abundance!* There is an abundant supply of love and health, which means there is also an abundant supply of success, money, and happiness to go around.

I want you to really get this point. You have been conditioned to believe in limitation. So, of course you're going to hear its voice when it whispers: "Don't brag about your success." "Don't show how talented you really are." "Don't take the credit you deserve." And that most annoying command of all: "Be humble."

Humble people never created a cure for a disease. Humble people don't start organizations like Mothers Against Drunk Driving or the Red Cross.

The only part humility plays in accomplishing something BIG is the humility before God in knowing He chose you, as He chooses each person, to fulfill a unique purpose. Now I encourage you to receive this truth in humility and go kick some ass!

It's not the voice of limitation that holds you back. It's how you manage that voice and the habit of giving it power that holds you back.

Let's get back to my story so you can see how I broke free...

So there I was, staring miserably at myself in the mirror of the ladies room, ten minutes away from addressing a huge crowd, hyperventilating and full of lack thinking. I did the only thing I know to do when faced with such a monster: I prayed. And somehow this thought came into my mind: "Good for her! Good for that speaker who is connecting so well with the audience. She is warming them up for the next great speaker...me! I am going to run up on stage and share my important message, because that's who I am.

"I too am a great speaker!"

There is enough "good speaker" to go around. There is enough "successful career" to go around. There is enough "great marriage" to go around. There is enough love, health, money, and success to go around because we live in a world of abundance!

Shift your belief and conquer the voice of limitation today by making this your mantra:

"We live in an abundant world. There is always more than enough!"

Write your own mantra about abundance here:

_____

_____

The Princess and Money

Why is it that so few women plan to be millionaires? Women take emotional risks all the time. Women take physical risks all the time. Why don't they take financial risks? Most women rent when we should buy. We think "jobs" when we should think "careers." And we lose several good years of saving or investing in our twenties while we're searching for Mr. Right!

Maybe it's because we've been programmed since birth, from our fairytales, novels, magazines, and television shows, to believe that men make the money and women marry into it.

Think of yourself when you were ten years old. Did you want to be a millionaire when you grew up? When you were a little girl playing with your dolls, did you play house where your mom doll went to work and built a million-dollar company? Hah! I can just see it now...

Two five-year-old little girls are playing with their Barbie collection when one of the little girls motions her Barbie to say, "Ken, guess what? My company's stock reached its highest level today. Let's go out and celebrate!" And the other little girl motions her Barbie to say, "We're opening up our seventh store next month in Paris! Do you want to invest in my company?"

Why don't little girls play business instead of house? The answer to this also answers the question: Why don't women plan to be millionaires—or billionaires?

Reality #1:
Our Families Didn't See Us as Millionaires.

Women rarely talk about how much money we make or what would be our best business strategy to create mega-wealth. People seem to think that when a man discusses earning strategies, he is being heroic—but they're not as comfortable when a woman does the same. Why is that?

Reality #2:
Our Society Doesn't See Us as Millionaires.

18

One reason our families don't see us as millionaires, is because, in general, our culture doesn't perceive women as rich and prosperous. True, as more women have succeeded, this view has shifted somewhat, but women as millionaires is not the predominant way our culture sees us.

I say this not to upset you or encourage you to get on the "They hold us back and they must pay!" bandwagon. I simply want you to know what you're dealing with. When you know the rules of the game you're playing, you can be far more successful.

So, if you want to be a millionaire or a billionaire, *you're first going to have to give yourself permission to do it!*

Let's do a little exercise. I want you to picture in your mind a rich person. Notice that person. Describe that person. Write the rich person's name here:

_____.

Now I want you to picture another rich person. Describe them. Notice as much as you can about them. Write the rich person's name here:

_____.

I want you to picture a third rich person. Notice that rich person. Again, describe as much about that person as possible. Write the rich person's name here:

_____.

Now, look back at your three people and ask yourself some revealing questions.

#1: Were you one of your three rich people? If not, why not? Until you see yourself as a rich person (even before you are), you won't even begin to attract it. Taking this small step of seeing yourself as wealthy (even before you are), is a powerful technique and supports the Law of Attraction that we'll talk about in a future chapter.

When you tell yourself you are a wealthy woman, your posture will be different. You'll walk more confidently. You'll handle challenge better. You'll treat people differently. And you'll begin attracting opportunities that will create wealth.

Really!

Incorporating this simple habit in your life creates huge results. Make a commitment to visualize yourself as a wealthy woman every day and repeat, "I am a wealthy woman!"

#2: Were your three rich people all celebrities? This reveals that your subconscious belief is that wealth is for the super-human, bigger-than-life kind of person, not regular, everyday folk like you and me. Shift this belief by doing some research. Find some wealthy women who live in your community, work in your industry, attend your church, or are members of your clubs. Invite them for coffee, interview them, and get to know them. See them as someone just like you—because they are.

#3: Were your three rich people men? This is also very revealing to where your subconscious belief is about women millionaires. While there are many men millionaires, the women millionaires count is growing like the morning Starbuck's line!

Now, some of you reading this may be saying, "Lisa, I want to be a woman millionaire or a billionaire, but I have a family and need to wait until the kids are out of the house." I've heard this statement many times and my response is this:

Creating wealth is a process.

Being a millionaire or a billionaire is a journey that you grow into. Begin the process now. Your path to developing wealth is a powerful and inspiring example to your children. It is completely your choice the speed at which you build your business and wealth. You may want to go fast and furious or you may choose the slower, steady path. Whichever you choose doesn't matter as much as just choosing one.

Get on the path to wealth development now, because doing so promises to be the best personal development program you will ever follow and the best example for your children. And no matter what speed you choose to take, *it all begins with you seeing yourself as a wealthy woman.*

Create the belief that you don't have to give up love or family to build a lucrative business, to become a millionaire or billionaire. This fear of the so-called lonely life we've been told career women face is a lie. According to Millionaire Women Next Door, the median age of women with seven-figure assets is forty-nine; nineteen out of twenty have been married and/or have children, and only about 20 percent are divorced. Most millionaire women are married with children and they created their wealth in their own entrepreneurial venture!

In the research I did for *Don't Mess With the Princess!* I read about some amazingly common entrepreneurial women who touched, moved, and inspired me by their incredible examples. Here are three stories of ordinary, everyday women just like you and me who built their fortunes through entrepreneurship.

The Leading (Less Famous) Women Entrepreneurs of the World

Cheryl Womack

Married and the mother of two, Cheryl Womack worked for an insurance company in the department that covered truckers. When her boss wouldn't let her take the next step in sales, she didn't just get mad about it, she did something. She said to herself, "If I can't be my own boss, I don't want to be in this business." Anger and unfair treatment motivated her to go out on her own. She started her own business—selling insurance to independent truckers—in her basement and grew her company while raising two children. That company, which she started with just $17,000 in 1983, sold for more than $100 million in 2002.

Cheryl now manages a nonprofit organization called "The Leading Women Entrepreneurs of the World," which helps others on their way up. Cheryl recently pledged $2 million to build a women's softball field at her alma mater, the University of Kansas.

Liz Elting

Liz Elting had a good job working in financial services, but she wasn't happy. One day she thought, "Why am I doing this? I don't love it. What I love is languages." Shortly after graduating with an MBA from New York University's business school, Liz started Trans-Perfect, an international translation and interpretation service, with a classmate. Their start-up investment: $5,000, largely from credit cards. Today her company has thirty branches, employs the most qualified linguists, and offers the fastest service in more than one hundred languages. And the business takes in more than $65 million a year.

Liz's toughest challenge so far came when she landed a major contract for a company who needed the translation of an 800-page geology study from English into Russian—in just six days! She needed to quickly find people with very specialized knowledge. Through networking, Liz located translators who had actually worked in the mines in Russia and flew them in to complete the job.

"We still have a long way to go as a company," Liz said in a recent interview. "But now I don't need to work on weekends, and I get to be home with my kids every night. And having a certain amount financially does make me feel secure. It's nice not to have to worry about money day in and day out."

Tina Wells

Tina's company, which keeps clients such as Sony and MGA Entertainment updated on the latest trends among young buyers, is worth more than $5 million. At the age of sixteen, she began writing product reviews for a small newspaper. One day Tina was talking to the director of marketing of a company for which she had written a report. The woman told Tina that she'd just paid someone $25,000 to do what she'd done—and that Tina had done it better. As Tina tells it, "I screamed, 'People get paid for this?'" She landed her first paying client her freshman year in college.

"Until I graduated," she says, "I had trouble getting taken seriously as a businesswoman. So I started putting out research that was different from what everybody else was doing: It was more informative, sexy, and scandalous. For instance, I wrote a report saying we interviewed five hundred kids, and 99 percent of them said they illegally downloaded music and were not going to stop.

We also did surveys on sex and religion, things people wanted to know about but were too scared to ask. We now have nine thousand teenage and young adult 'buzzspotters' who scope out what their peers are thinking and doing." Tina made a choice at the beginning of her career to, as she states, "Do what men do and make the money!"

Success Is a Choice

The process of creating success and the path to wealth begins when you decide. Have you decided yet? You don't have to give up love or family when you decided to be wealthy; you just have to deicide and then trust that you will be divinely guided to keep yourself and your family in balance while you're building your wealth.

So I ask you: Are you ready to step onto the path of wealth? Do you give yourself permission to be a wealthy woman entrepreneur? What do you choose and by when do you want to accomplish it? Write your declaration here:

_____

_____

_____

Now that you have chosen to step on the path of building wealth, and you see yourself as a wealthy woman, what do you want to do with all that wealth when you manifest it?

A big reason why some people sabotage their success is they do not plan how they will spend their money or what kind of lifestyle they will live when they manifest their wealth, and they become lost! It's not the money that causes sabotage; it's the lack of clarity and direction.

23

Think of how many celebrities get rich, then crash and burn. And we make up our minds that money ruins you. But make no mistake, it's not the money in itself that destroys people, but their own decisions about what to do with it. That's why it is mandatory to focus on the woman you are developing into from creating your wealth, not the wealth itself. It is important to know how you will live when you manifest your dream.

When you attract wealth and you become a millionaire/billionaire, how will you live? How will your family live?

_____

_____

_____

What are your core values that money will enhance?

_____

_____

_____

What is your contribution to the planet that money can expand?

_____

_____

_____

What is your purpose that money will enhance?

_____

_____

_____

When you have clarity on how you and your family will live after you attract your wealth, you will live into that vision. When you

24

realize how wealth can enhance your purpose, core values, and contribution to the planet, you'll stay centered and maintain a healthy internal balance. And, you'll conquer the limiting money beliefs that most people hold.

Shatter the Most Common Negative Money Beliefs

1. Money Is Bad / Dangerous

I've heard well-meaning people quote Scripture and wildly proclaim, "Money is the root of all evil." Well, that sure decides it. I mean, who wants to have anything to do with THE ROOT OF EVIL!? Not me! But that's not what Scripture says at all. That wonderful verse reads, "The LOVE of money is the root of all evil." In its true definition, love in this verse means "the consistent pursuit of," which describes someone who would deny his or her own child to get money. That person is evil and deserves everything this verse implies.

But you are not that person—not even close! (And if you are, then what the heck are you doing reading one of my books? It just might melt in your hands!)

Truth: **Money Gives You Choices**

The reality about money is it gives you the choice to help yourself and others. It offers the opportunity to contribute in powerful ways. And the more money you make, the more you can contribute! My hope is you—the reader of "Don't Mess With the Princess!"—will manifest billions of dollars and be in the position to greatly help yourself, your family, your community, and the world. I believe you were born to be blessed—richly blessed—to be a blessing to others!

2. Money Changes You

Let's face it, we have some pretty bad role models of wealthy people. We see it in the media, movies, and on the Internet. We hear the stories about rich celebrities, rock stars, business moguls, and pro athletes wreaking havoc and leaving destruction in their wake. And we think (even if it's subconsciously), "Money makes people do crazy things" or "Money will make me a bad person." And then we make a decision to not have any part of money.

You may make this decision consciously, but it's more likely you make it on the subconscious level—and the most dangerous choice is the one made subconsciously. You make a judgment about rich people and a subconscious decision not to be one of them. What happens is you immediately begin the process of sabotaging your success, even though externally you say you want to be wealthy! All because you are deceived, uneducated, and you don't discern! Hold that thought for just a minute and consider this...

We also have stories of celebrities, rock stars, business moguls, and pro athletes who contribute in major ways. They donate time and money to their communities and countless charities, often writing checks for multimillions to build orphanages, schools, healthcare facilities, and community centers. However, the negative examples always stay in our mind—and get reported far more often than the positive examples!

You've got to ask yourself, "Why is that?"

Something else I want you to consider is this: What causes some wealthy people to act in a generous way, while others act in a destructive way? Was it the money itself that caused that choice? Of course not. A person who becomes rich is the same person he or she was BEFORE the wealth appeared.

Truth: **Money Doesn't Change You. Money Makes You More of Who You Already Are!**

If you start out a jerk, then when you come into money, you will just be a big fat jerk—with the capacity to earn the title of "Biggest Jerk of All Time"! And in the same way, if you're a kind, generous person and you come into money, you will become an even kinder, more generous person!

26

You will see that newfound wealth as an opportunity to do more than you have done already. You will be the kind of person who builds libraries and daycare centers and art galleries, the kind of person who donates millions to find cures, feed starving babies, heal the violated, and comfort the underprivileged. You'll do this because you have a heart of a giver and you have the means (the money) to do it!

3. Wealthy People Constantly Think About Their Wealth

I used to think that money was difficult to manage and would take too much of my time to invest it and supervise it. And I used that limiting belief to keep me from attracting wealth. I had the belief that all wealthy people did was talk about and manage their fortune. I couldn't have been more deceived! In fact, I thought about money far more when I was broke than I do now that I am wealthy! It used to be all I thought about. I would wake up in the morning, call the automated teller at my bank, and find out which checks went through so I'd know whether I had to rush down to make a deposit before any of them bounced. Thoughts of money (or the lack of it) consumed me!

Now that I am wealthy, I think about money far less. I have competent people in place to manage my real estate investments and my stock portfolio. All I have to do is oversee it. I never have to decide which bills will get paid this month or worry whether checks will be returned, stamped in red with those nasty letters, "NSF." What freedom! It has cleared my mind from so much concern and unending worry.

Believe me, I can still remember all the energy I used to expel on worrying whether I could pay my bills. Never again! Being wealthy gives me the space, time, and choice to live my purpose and my life to the highest level. Do you know how good it feels to see a need in your community and be able to fill it? Do you know how empowering it is to be able to generously give when you're asked? It's the most wonderful feeling ever! And I want that same feeling for you.

So stop thinking small. Stop being small. Your being small is not serving anyone! If anything, it is hurting the people around you who need you to have the faith to step out, to see yourself as the wealthy woman you are, and to grow your company to create the most wealth possible. Then, enjoy a life of contribution in the most profound ways!

Truth: **Money Gives You Freedom**

Three Habits to Implement Every Day—Starting Today:
1. Give yourself permission to be a millionaire/billionaire.
2. Believe that becoming wealthy is doable.
3. Visualize yourself as a wealthy woman NOW.

Mantra:

"It's fun being a millionaire/billionaire! It's good for my family, my community, my world for me to be a millionaire/billionaire! It's easy to attract wealth!"

Create your own mantra about money:

_____

_____

_____

Are you too nice? In the next chapter, you'll learn how to break through the limiting and dangerous belief "Girls Are Sugar and Spice and Everything Nice!"

"Dreams come a size too big so that we can grow into them."

—Josie Bissett

Chapter 2

Sugar and Spice and Everything Nice

Janet was sharing with me a memory she had from childhood of her mother introducing her to one of their new neighbors. When Janet didn't shake the man's hand, her mother got angry and said, "Janet, don't be rude."

Carol, who loved to climb trees and wrestle with her brothers, was told by a well-meaning teacher that girls were to act like 'little ladies'.

Jennifer felt her father's disapproval when she wanted to compete in the third grade soccer tournament instead of the town's beauty pageant.

The stories are countless and the message is clear:

Girls are supposed to be sweet because they are made of "Sugar and Spice and Everything Nice."

Well, what is nice? Is it nice to yell at your two-year-old just before she runs out in the street? Is it nice to start an organization called, *Mother's Against Drunk Driving* and be a powerful force for drug-free motorists? Is it nice to stand up to a man who beats you, put him in jail and say, "Never again!"

The 'Be Nice' syndrome shows up for women in the boardroom, the family room, and the bedroom. Let's first talk about women in the boardroom (Unless you want to skip ahead to women in the bedroom!)

Nice Girls in the Boardroom

What are the rules for a woman in the boardroom? Whether that woman is leading the company or just presenting her ideas, she first has to know without doubt that she belongs there. She must believe with fervent conviction her contribution is important ~ even vital to the success of the company. The unconscious belief still exists that "It's a Man's World". Women hold the power to shift this belief by simply not participating in it! It's not real. It's a lie created centuries ago. And the only way to keep the lie alive is to believe in it. As soon as you choose not to participate in this lie, it vanishes. Poof! Just like that.

What I'm about to say may shock you, but according to my research, it's not men who are holding women back in the boardroom, in relationship, or in life. It is women and the prevailing, subconscious belief that they aren't supposed to be there.

I mean let's face it, it is relatively new to our culture, economy, and industry to have women leaders. Here are the startling facts:

The Constitution, as it was originally written, didn't let women vote in federal elections. Beginning in the mid-19th century, groups of women began lecturing, marching, and lobbying for the right to vote. The first women's rights convention took place in 1848, this became known as the Women's Suffrage Movement, and it lasted 72 years!

It wasn't until 1920, when the 19th amendment passed, that women finally had the right to vote.

Woman in the boardroom is a relatively new reality. It was the 1970's when my Aunt Cori, a single mom of three children, worked as a manager at Keiser and led nearly 100 people. This was not 'the norm'. And she felt it. Most of her female friends were homemakers. That was just 40 years ago!

It is a prevailing fact that it's relatively new to have a woman in leadership roles. But that doesn't mean we apologize or quit. It just means we acknowledge what we're dealing with here and do what we can to create opportunity for more women in leadership.

As we talked about in Chapter One: You, as a Princess, have the power to put an end to, "It's a man's world" and create, "It's a human being world" through your thoughts, beliefs, and actions.

If you want to have a leadership position in your place of work or you dream of running your own business, the first step is to believe that you can! And you do that by being fiercely committed to having empowering thoughts, beliefs and actions relating to women in leadership. If you want a leadership position in your corporation, or you want to begin your own entrepreneurial venture, then declare it! Envision it! Celebrate it! And take action to manifest it!

But that begs the question, "Do women have what it takes to successfully lead in the boardroom?"

Are Women Wired for Business?

Are women cut out to be entrepreneurs? Do they have what it takes to make it in a business culture that has been designed, cultivated, and run by men?

This is one of those questions that defy a quick and clear answer. But, sift through all the statistics, weigh the anecdotal evidence, and you can't help but come to the conclusion that... Well, keep reading.

First, let's talk about motivation. What is the driving force behind why men and why women become entrepreneurs. According to research done by Robert D. Hisrich, a professor of entrepreneurship at Case Western Reserve University in Cleveland, there is very little difference between the sexes and what drives them.

He refers to a broad-based study that looked at entrepreneurial motivation by gender in which they discovered the driving force behind entrepreneurship.

The top three reasons for men are:
1.   Independence
2.   The chance to make lots of money
3.   Enthusiasm for the idea behind the business

The top three reasons for women are:
1.   Independence
2.   Enthusiasm for the idea behind the business
3.   The chance to make lots of money

You may be thinking to yourself; "So what? Why are you even bringing this up, Lisa?" Well, I include this study in this chapter to prove an important fact. Both women and men are human and have the same human wants, needs, and desires. And as for having the drive and motivation needed in business, women are just as programmed for success in an entrepreneurial venture as men. The core satisfactions that come from entrepreneurialism are cross-gender.

In other words, women are inherent entrepreneurs; to be a part of the business world is a natural and normal role for them. And the business world reflects this. The increase in women entrepreneurs over the past decade has been nothing short of amazing, as women make up for lost time. Consider this:

- According to a 2001 report by the Small Business Administration's Office of Advocacy, in the latter part of the 1990s, the number of women-owned businesses increased by 16 percent and their revenue by 33 percent compared to the first part of the decade.
- Over the past several years, women created 1.5 million sole proprietorships, outpacing their male counterparts by 25 percent, according to another Office of Advocacy study released in 2003.

Women are finding great fulfillment in entrepreneurialism because they are wired for it. Let's now take a look at how entrepreneurialism actually fits best for the way a woman is wired.

How Women Are Wired
for Success in Business

1. Women are wired to be phenomenal multitaskers:

When it comes to keeping up the pace of new-business creation, women are wired for success. Women have a tremendous capability to multitask and focus on several things at once—and they do it quite well. In fact, this capability is so ingrained in their being, I believe women commonly attract drama and problems in their life to keep them engaged in multi-tasking and managing several issues at once. (We'll talk more about this and how to deal with the dangers of it in a later chapter.)

2. Women are wired with emotion and empathy

Most women choose "lifestyle businesses". These are enterprises based on personal interests and passions. The other entrepreneurial ventures women choose tend to be in the service industry, because they love people and are wired to nurture and take care of them. According to research, a full 70 percent of the income earned by female-owned businesses are in the service sector. Women generally choose enterprises that play to their strengths. They are led by their passion and maintain the clarity of that passion with ease. They are innately able to empathize with their employees and clients. Women often have incredible insight and capability in marketing and management.

3. Women are wired to deal with conflict resolution

An ability to empathize with people both inside and outside their companies makes women, on average, excellent managers (and marketers). It also may be why they gravitate to the service industries, which often require personal interaction with clients. By nature, women are wired to seek resolution and use this intrinsic ability to resolve disputes and divergence and create community. Women are natural diplomats.

4. Women are wired with an instinct and intuition

Remember the movie What Women Want with Mel Gibson? His character portrayed a man who could read a woman's mind. Women have a similar aptitude; intuition and instinct. Women are wired to Listen to their gut feeling; they have a good sense of what is really going on, what the real needs are, and who is best qualified to fulfill them. In a way, a woman can read the minds of her customers, her market, and her employees when she taps into her power of intuition.

5. Women are wired to work as a team

Yes, we will "ask for directions"! And according to research, women are wired to ask for help, build support, and create a team to give her a strong basis for long-term success in business. While women still can have an occasional ego trip and catty discourse, overall they are most apt to grow and maintain close community with employees and clients.

These five innate talents are powerful forces to ensure success in business. However, make no mistake, as compelling as these innate abilities are, they can also be the very reason a woman fails in business and life. When a woman relies too heavily on any one of these five inherent gifts, she tends to get out of balance and, if not monitored, will destroy the very business she's trying to build. The following are the most common pitfalls:

1. Multitasking

Women have a tendency to do too much. Heal yourself from martyr mentality by hiring an assistant immediately. From the time you start up a business, you'll need assistance, even if it's part-time. And remember, your help should grow as your business grows. Delegate! You will conquer the martyr mentality by scheduling regular massages, workouts, and time off. You can't pour out of an empty pitcher! Fill yourself up regularly. It benefits everyone around you.

2. Emotion and Empathy

When you're finding yourself more concerned with helping people than you are about your bottom line, it's time to have a strong conversation with yourself about the major importance of being profitable. Keep your eye on the bottom line. Hire someone who is financially savvy and review your P & L (profit and loss) statement monthly. No one's going to "heal the world" if you're not making money and being profitable in business.

3. Conflict Resolution

When you start cutting out articles for an employee on "How to Save Your Marriage," you know you've gone too far. Women can fall into the trap of caring too much about their employees' problems. When you find yourself playing counselor or mom-of-the-year to your employees, stop and realize you're doing it out of your own desire to be needed. Your employees need you to be the leader that you are. Keep yourself from being drawn too deeply into your employees' lives.

4. Instinct and Intuition

I realize there is a danger of following your intuition without consulting what is actually fact, or even refusing to believe that the facts are true. However, as I sit here writing this chapter, 35,000 feet above the planet on my way to Tahiti, I realize it's been my intuition and instinct that have propelled my career and put me in the first class seat in which I sit. I can't see any downfall of tapping into your intuition. Especially since I believe most womendon't utilize the power of intuition enough! So what I'll say is, follow your passion, tap into your intuition, and if you realize a pitfall, e-mail me and let me know. I'll include it in the next version of, Don't Mess With the Princess!

5. Teamwork

Building a team is vital to business success. The danger to seeking other people's help only comes if you aren't valuing your own. In other words, if you have to consult with 7,214 people before you can make a decision... or you have to read zillions of books to make sure you have all the information before you can venture out on your own... or if you give all the credit to another and devalue your own worth, you are out of balance. Ask for help, seek guidance, get assistance, but never at the cost of devaluing or distrusting yourself or your own ability.

With your innate abilities to multitask, stay in touch with emotion, draw on conflict resolution, tap into instinct and intuition, build strong teams, and balance all of these gifts with the truth that you are wired for business, you have what it takes to build strong, sovereign, successful companies.

Hiring a business coach will help you maintain balance and keep you accountable to creating success in work and in life. If you want to greatly improve your productivity, maintain balance, and improve your profits, check out my Quantum Leap Coaching Program and Rich Life Mastermind Retreats at www.RichLifeMastermindRe-treat.com.

You are a woman. And women are wired for business. You don't have to 'act like a man' in the boardroom to be successful. Conversely, you don't have to be a 'nice girl' in the boardroom. You are a women and you are wired for business. You bring a unique and powerful set of gifts and talents that are unique to women. Don't allow anyone's belief or mindset to silence the truth that you have everything you need—right now—to build a successful business venture; because as a woman, you are wired for it!

Nice Girls in the Family Room

Don't you just love hosting elegant dinner parties? Your perfect husband helps you clean your perfect home. Your perfect outfit fits great and you are perfectly ready on time. Your perfectly behaved children offer your guests perfectly cooked appetizers that you prepared in your perfect kitchen earlier in the day during your daily 'family time'... which of course is always perfect!

Ha! Ya, right!

I don't know about you, but the last time I hosted an elegant dinner party without it being catered, Ronald Reagan was president!

If you are left exhausted, resentful, or angry with any of the responsibilities that you have as a wife and mom, then maybe it's time to evaluate your beliefs and ask yourself, "Are they best for me and my family?"

A Princess doesn't have to prove anything to herself or others. When she chooses to host a party or when she makes family dinners or drive to the soccer field for the 79th time, she does it, not out of obligation or because it makes her look good; she does it because she wants to and it brings her joy.

You have the power to shift the atmosphere in your home by finding joy in taking care of your home and your family. But please, Princess, realize this: You can't find the joy of giving if you are empty, exhausted, and stressed.

If that describes you, have a conversation with your family. Tell the truth. Ask for help. Make a list of all the jobs that are part of running a great home and delegate them to your kids or hire them out. You as the woman of your home create the tone in the home. If you have the belief that you are 'supposed' to do it all and that is expected of you, you're wrong and it's not best for anyone!

Stop trying to be Super Woman!

When you are in the habit of 'doing it all' it is a reflection of low self esteem. Doing it all actually gives you the feeling that you are important and needed. What are you still trying to prove? Think about it!

And when you refuse to delegate to your children, you are steeling their opportunity to build their self-esteem. When you don't delegate household jobs to your children, the message you are sending is clear: You secretly believe they can't do it by themselves or at least not as good as you can.

Put an end to the control!

Give up your need to be needed

It was almost midnight when the phone rang. It was Peter calling to confirm our arrival time for our flight. When I told him I was still packing for myself and the kids, he said, "Lisa, when are you going to let the kids do things for themselves?"

"I don't know," I answered. But secretly I did know. I didn't let my kids do for themselves because of two reasons: Doing everything for my kids made me feel like I was a good mom. And, doing everything for my kids meant it would be done 'right'!

Through that conversation with Peter, I began to see the destructive habit I was creating. I was actually disempowering my children by doing so much for them.

What about you?

Do you believe moms are supposed to do all the cooking, wash the kid's clothes, be their chauffer, their housekeeper, and their alarm clock? Do those things make you feel needed? And are you secretly addicted to the need to be needed?

There are three choices you have in your role as a mom. They are:

Smotherhood;
Otherhood; and
Motherhood.

Smotherhood: You do everything for your children because you believe that's what good moms do. You have a secret need to be needed and get this need met by smothering your children.

Otherhood: You are resigned when it comes to being a mom. You don't care about teaching responsibility, discipline, or love. Your mind, focus and desire is on other interests.

Motherhood: You are full and complete within yourself. When you prepare a meal or drive your child to soccer, you do it, not because you have to or it's expected of you, but because you want to. It brings you joy to watch your children grow up and take on more and more responsibility of their own. They need you less and less every day.

Which one are you? Are you willing to sit down and have a serious talk with yourself? Consider where you need to shift your beliefs of what a "great mom" is. Consider where you are still maintaining the role of Super Mom.

You know what the job description is of a great mom? It's a woman who puts herself out of a job!

Great moms, great dads put themselves out of a job. They do less and less for their growing child until one day they wake up and they're just not needed anymore. They retire from being the parent.

Stop reading for just a second and notice what you are thinking and feeling right now. Did you feel a bolt of fear come up your spine when you read the words, "You will retire from being a mom because you're just not needed anymore"?

Tell the truth, even just to yourself. Many woman find their identity in their children. Without their kids they don't know who they are! But you are not really a mom. You are a force of energy. Period. And one of the roles you chose in your life is being a mom. Don't get so attached to the labels we use in life. And be cautious not to gain your identity in your children or their success. It hurts your child when you live vicariously through them. The best thing you can do for your kids is have a life! Be the unique, wonderful, force of energy that you are and continue to develop your uniqueness even during the years you have children in your care.

So, I ask you, are you willing to put structures in place where you're on the path of retiring? Empower you children, let them do for themselves, and begin to put yourself out of a job.

Breakthrough the 'Meaning Syndrome'

Lydia studied graphic design and always wanted to be a set designer for Broadway. It was a life-long dream. But the dream never happened. So instead of Broadway she went into furniture design and dabbled in local theater. Then one day Lydia got a call. A college friend was moving to London to design the staging for an upcoming musical. She asked Lydia if she would accept the one year contract and come to London with her.

Lydia was thrilled. But when she began sharing the news with her friends and family, they were shocked that Lydia was even considering it because she had two children. Lydia made a common mistake: she placed a 'meaning' to her actions. If Lydia accepted the opportunity and moved her family to London for a year, it means she's a bad mom. And if Lydia declines the one-year contact, it means she's a good mom.

I met Lydia last month at one of my speaking engagements. It's been 13 years since she declined the London opportunity. She smiled as she spoke of her grown children and seemed content with her choice made so many years ago.

But I couldn't help but wonder... What if? What if Lydia had said yes to the dream and moved her children and husband to London for a year?

Her kids would have seen a side of culture and the Arts that few ever do. They would have traveled to neighboring countries and experienced different traditions, languages, and people. And they would have had the incredible privilege of watching their mom achieve her dream and give it right back to each of them.

What about you?

Where are you keeping yourself from your dreams because you think you are being noble? Where are you holding yourself back because you have a belief that it means you're a terrible mom or a bad wife?

Your husband and your children love you. And loving people find great joy in supporting those they love. Have a conversation with your family. Tell the truth about your dreams and what each of them can do to support you in achieving them.

See your spouse and your children as supportive. If you don't think they are, their 'resistance' could be created by you. I used to hide behind the belief that my family was not supportive of me, too. It kept me small and safe. But it was a lie! Breakthrough this resistance and fear by sharing your dreams and your conviction to accomplishing your goals. Then work together to achieve those dreams and become a unified contribution to the world.

When You're Healthy and Wealthy, Everyone Wins!

I can still remember the first time I involved my children in a money goal I had for the month. "I have an announcement to make," I proclaim as I sat down to dinner with my three children. There was no response, just bewildered stares. I continued...

"Mom made a lot of money this month," I said, revealing my secret. "And I want to share it with you."

I began to tell them all the things they do to help me build my business. "You take care of yourself and don't complain when I leave for work," I said. "You do the grocery shopping and help me prepare our dinners. And you get your own clothes ready for school everyday." The list went on and on.

"This was a really big month for me," I concluded. "And I want to give you some of what I earned—whatever amount you want."

Well, their eyes opened up like windows on a cool spring day, and for the next ten minutes they expressed their thoughts on how much they thought they should each get.

First, Auriana, my seventeen year old daughter, spoke up, "I think you should give me however much you want to give," she stated. (What a diplomat!)

Connor chimed in, "I think you should give me ten dollars!" (I need to help him raise his expectations.)

Then, it was Beau's turn. "I think I should get anywhere between 50 and 100 dollars." he replied confidently.

After listening to all of their thoughts, I took out three one-hundred dollar bills and placed one in front of each of my kids.

"Wow!" Auriana said as she picked up the bill. "Thanks, mom!" Beau replied, with a big smile on his face. "I've never even seen a hundred dollar bill before!" Connor shouted.

What a feeling! That experience was the first of many times I was able to richly give. I will never tire of creating wealth and then sharing it with the people I love the most.

What about your beliefs? Do you share the Law of Abundance with your children? Or do they always see you tired or complaining about work? Do you show your children that you take care of yourself by healthy eating, resting when you're tired, working out, treating yourself to manicures and massage? Do your children know not to disturb you when you're involved your meditation time or prayer time?

You aren't serving anyone by not taking care of yourself and then thinking that you are somehow being noble!

Begin being fiercely committed to taking care of yourself. Schedule your quiet time, workouts, healthy treats, and social time. Talk to your kids about your Big Dream and involve them in helping you achieve it. Post your Dream Board in your home and share it with your children. Let them be a part of creating your health, your wealth, and achieving your dreams. You are your child's greatest example. If you want them to experience abundant, faith-filled lives, then do it first for yourself. They will learn the Law of Abundance best through watching you living it!

When you're healthy, wealthy, and whole, everyone wins!

Nice Girls in the Bedroom

Do you love having sex? Are you sexually satisfied and experience multiple orgasms? If you're a married woman, I hope you can say "Yes! Yes! Yes!"

Sex in marriage is one of the most phenomenal gifts God created for us. Sex will unify you as a couple, boost your vitality, lower your stress level, increase your respect for each other, improve your communication and... did I mention it unifies you as a couple!

I've interviewed over 100 married men and what I discovered is husbands want so desperately to please their wives sexually, but most don't have a clue what their wife's sexual fantasies are.

Culture, religion, and prevailing negative beliefs have told woman that their sexual desires are not important. The focus of our culture has been the sexual satisfaction of men.

But this is not the focus or the general belief held by the husbands I interviewed. These men were all very interested in pleasing their wife and felt incredible satisfaction knowing how to do that! And they need your help.

Give yourself permission to explore your own body, know what you like, and share that with your husband; the man who loves you so much and wants to satisfy you sexually.

Also, know that most men will not take initiative to ask you. Maybe it's their ego that doesn't let them admit that they can't read your mind (or your body) and they really don't know how to give you what you want sexually. Don't be afraid to ask for what you want in bed.

Help him out, okay? Have a conversation with him and share your sexual desires and fantasies with him. Hint: You can invite him to take a Tantra Sex class together or invest in the book, "The Tantra Sex Weekend" by Lana Holstein and David Taylor.

All this talk about sex leads me to the conversation about sex and dating...

Think twice before you fall into the general belief that casual sex is just casual sex. There's no such thing as casual sex. When you choose to have sex with a man who you haven't built a relationship with, your ability to create a healthy and whole relationship is impaired. Give yourself and your new relationship the gift of time. Hold a higher standard for yourself. You're worth it!

This topic is important to the *Don't Mess With the Princess!* message. So we will continue our conversation in the chapter 8. For now, go fix yourself a latte or a tea, kick back in a comfy place and let's talk about the power in accepting "what is" and being open to manifesting what's possible!

"If one is lucky, a solitary fantasy can totally transform one million realities."

—May Angelou

Chapter 3

C'est Comme ça

Accepting What Is

"It's an offer I can't refuse," I told Randy Gage during one of our Mastermind calls. I had just been offered the position of principal at a local Christian preschool, and wonderful visions of what lay ahead were already dancing through my head.

I pictured the students, learning, growing, and enjoying school under my direction. I saw myself giving a smile and a welcoming hug to each one as they walked into class every morning. I heard the teachers sharing their ideas with me on how we could make our school better. I felt the parents patting me on the back and shaking my hand in congratulation on a job well done...

My pleasant reverie was interrupted by Randy's voice coming over the phone.

"This isn't what you're meant to do," he counseled. "You are a professional speaker. You are a messenger."

"But this might just be the time for me to get back to my first career—teaching," I argued. "I could finally use my degree in school leadership." I continued to enthuse about what I saw as a great opportunity.

But Randy wasn't buying it.

"Okay," I said, switching gears, "I'll do both then."

Again Randy remained unmoved, instead launching into a detailed explanation of my faulty logic and how I was being seduced by the dark side of a regular paycheck. After a grueling couple of hours, although for some reason the hands of the clock said only ten minutes, we ended our conversation with my promise to think more about it before making a decision.

That weekend, I attended the National Speakers Association convention, where I was scheduled to give a presentation to members on how to build their speaking business. Little did I know I had a date with destiny.

When I walked into the hotel, I immediately noticed another convention was being held there that weekend—for the Principals Association! Throughout my entire stay, all of my conversations were either with a public speaker or a principal. Talking with the principals rekindled my memory of some of the reasons why I had left teaching: the bureaucracy of the educational system, the mounds of paperwork, and the long hours. (Somehow I had conveniently forgotten these aggravations.)

Then, during my presentation, I received another jolt. In the middle of my talk, a man raised his hand with a question.

"What do you do when you are torn between two careers?" he asked. "Do you think I can build a successful speaking career if I'm working at another job?"

His question stopped me cold. Could he read my mind? (To this day, I think Randy must have set him up!) But what surprised me even more was my response to him. It seemed as though God was speaking to him through me and at the same time directing the answer—with great precision—right to my heart.

"You can't serve two masters," I replied. "One will always suck the energy from the other." The next thing I knew I was telling my audience about the principal opportunity and how I was coming to realize a liberating truth:

I choose to have the courage to let go of things that keep me from my ultimate good.

We spent the next several minutes of the presentation in deep confession, as we all worked through a tough exercise: pruning. If you are a gardener you know the importance of pruning.

Pruning is getting rid of "stuff" that keeps you from what you really want. I'm not speaking here about just the evident harmful stuff. Pruning takes place when you get rid of seemingly "good stuff."

The "good stuff" is anything that looks like its enhancing your career and life but is actually holding you back. And when you are willing to prune these things, cutting them out of your life, you get what you really want.

After the presentation that day, we had a special excursion at a vineyard in Napa Valley. The vineyard owner gave a presentation on how to produce the best grapes.

"To harvest the best possible crop, you must be willing to cut the stalks way back so the sun can reach the inner layer of grapes, where the juiciest grapes grow," he said. "It's all in the pruning," he added as he grabbed a huge chunk of the stock and began chopping it off. We all started to laugh as we watched perfectly good grapes fall to the ground, knowing he was demonstrating the Pruning Principle I had taught in the program earlier that day.

So, what about you?

When was the last time you took out the machete in your life and cut back all those activities, people, thoughts, and beliefs that keep you from producing your best?

Get out your machete and consider what your business and personal life would look like if you did some pruning on the following "good activities":

Do you need to prune busyness and too much activity? It will make room for focused energy.

Do you need to stop making so many prospecting calls and make room for more follow-up calls?

Do you need to prune the habit of giving too much of your time and attention to a new consultant, an employee, or your child? This will open up the opportunity for them to be autonomous.

Do you need to prune your conversations? You talk so much in your presentations that you talk your prospect out of the sale!

The "good stuff" may be a word you overuse and now lacks power and becomes annoying and distracting!

Just like the gardener who must cut away a great portion of a plant, you need to be willing to cut out habits, activities, people, busyness, and even the stuff that may look good but actually keeps you from your ultimate good.

Are you ready to do some pruning in your life? Great! Make a list of the things in your life you need to cut out (even those seemingly "good" things):

_____

_____

_____

_____

_____

_____

Pruning—it's a liberating concept. Pruning is a habit you consciously choose to incorporate into your life. But what about those things in life you didn't want to let go of? What do you do when you have something taken from you, such as a loss of a job, a loss of a child, or, in my case, the loss of a marriage?

Surrender: Rising Above the Mind

I sat there speechless...

My husband walked into my office and told me he was moving out. I stopped breathing. My mind went reeling, trying to think of something to say. I felt like a bomb had exploded in the perfect garden I had planted and cultivated for the past eighteen years.

I knew there was only one thing to do. I had to do whatever it took to keep this from happening. For the next six weeks I read every book ever written on saving a marriage. I was determined and would not give up. My thoughts bounced wildly from "How could this be happening to me?" to "This is the best for me" and back to "How could this be happening to me?"

After months of turmoil, my counselor, who fully supported my "loyalty" to marriage, said to me, "Lisa, is Mark receptive to your actions?"

"No," I replied, "he cringes every time I talk about fighting for the marriage."

She looked at me and carefully said, "Could you be making it worse by holding on so tightly and not releasing this?"

I didn't reply.

"As much as I believe in marriage," the counselor continued, "the best thing is for you to let go, stop forcing the issue, and live in peace."

While I admit both Mark and I had not been happy together for a while, the thought of "giving up" on marriage and "giving in" to divorce was unfathomable. Even though I knew I was causing great pain in all of us by holding on so strongly, I just couldn't align divorce with my belief system.

I walked out of that counseling appointment angry with her suggestion and more determined than ever to make my marriage work.

Release Control to Receive

Later that day I had an appointment with Ellen, one of my personal coaching clients. She told me of the struggle she has experienced since she resigned from her eighteen-year career as a nurse. She had always wanted to be a nurse and saw herself only as a nurse. The thought of not being one any longer gave her pain.

I understood the cause of Ellen's turmoil came from the loss of her identity. Being a nurse defined her. And if her whole identity was in that label, *who would she be if she wasn't a nurse?*

I thought about what Ellen said for a long time after our coaching call. I realized I was just like her. So much of my identity was tied up in being a wife. No wonder I found it nearly impossible to let go.

I would be letting go of something in which I had placed my identity.

If I wasn't a wife, my husband's partner in life, the center of my happy, whole family, who was I?

The shocking reality set in when I admitted I was holding on to my marriage more out of a need of the familiar than dedication and love.

Ouch. The inconceivable had become a reality. I was part of the cause behind my troubled marriage and inevitable divorce. I wanted to blame Mark, saying he was an ass. I wanted to blame marriage, saying it's an outdated institution. I wanted to blame God, saying He had let us down.

But the truth was evident: A part of me wanted the divorce, too. I just didn't have the courage to admit it—let alone instigate it. My dogmatic beliefs shouted at me to stay married even though I knew we were not compatible—and that incompatibility was slowly suffocating each of us.

All my behaviors of fighting for my marriage looked noble. They felt noble. But in reality I was really fighting for the familiar, the "right" way to live. I fought more to hold on to my identity and keep the family together for the children, than out of love or the desire to be married. The rise of freedom came when I found the courage to admit the truth about my desire to be single and that this desire was valid and worthy of being voiced. But how could my family ever work if Mark and I were divorced and living in two separate homes?

Then, one day, my daughter Auriana helped me realize a beautiful possibility...

It had been a year since Mark moved out and the divorce was in the final stages. The kids and I were moving into our new home. I sat in the car, waiting to pick them up from school, when my cell phone rang. It was Steve, the painter. He had just finished painting the family room a bold, brilliant blue. I thought it would look gorgeous with the canary yellow sofas. But he felt the room needed something to tie it all together. That's why he was calling.

"I found it!" he shouted into the phone. "I found a piece of art in your garage that looks perfect with the blue wall and the yellow sofas. It pulls the whole room together."

He said it looked like some artist had painted the piece of art just for this room. I knew right away what piece of art he was talking about—the abstract I had painted with my artist friend Linda Richichi. My dear friend Linda had done a healing exercise with me through this painting. The exercise is a way to express your emotions through art to help you breakthrough pain and create healing.

In the middle of my piece of art, I painted a large circle that represented Mark, our kids, and me. The circle of my family was so large, I had to paint it on two canvases. The two canvases needed to be placed right up close together to make the circle whole.

When I walked into my new home and saw that Steve had hung the two canvases with a three-inch space in between, I was shocked. Even though it looked so perfect in that room, I couldn't help but realize the circle had been broken—my family had been broken! I began to cry and said, "The circle is broken. The circle is really broken!"

Then, my daughter Auriana hugged me and said, "Oh, Mom, the circle isn't broken. It's just bigger."

Wow! It's just bigger...

I smiled up at the painting and realized for the first time my family isn't broken. It still exists. It's just bigger. My family lives in two houses. And one day this family will be open to the possibility of bringing in another man and another woman with their entire families, which would make the circle even bigger.

"It's just more people to love!" Auriana said as she put her head on my shoulder.

My beautiful, loving daughter, who is full of possibility, was my healer and helped me receive what is and accept it for what it is...the wonderful possibility for something new!

That was the day I changed my belief about what had happened. Mark and I did not "break up," we just transformed our relationship into something new. That was the first day I was proud of my new self, of Mark, our new family, and all of our future possibilities.

It's been over three years now.

Today, I am a healthy, powerful woman who wakes up every morning excited about living my life. *The main cause of my healing came from surrendering and accepting "what is."*

When I finally surrendered to receiving things just as they were and just as they were not–without judgment–a healing occurred. And I could begin to see all the wonderful possibility available for us as a "family who lives in two houses."

I am committed to being friends with my former husband. That's why I don't label Mark an "ex-husband." He is my former husband or my first husband. That's why I speak highly of him. And I never call him when I'm feeling angry or mean. I know those feelings still come up and it's up to me not to let them get out of control.

If you are divorced, use my family as living proof that it is possible to create whatever you want for yourself, your former spouse, and your children. You just have to choose to surrender and accept what is. This is a life of integrity. This is a life based on truth. And this life is a powerful contribution to the planet.

So, what about you?

Are you holding on to a title, a job, a habit, a relationship, or a prospect you know is not in your best interest, but you don't have the courage to let go?

Maybe you've been doing it that way for so long and so much of your identity is tied up in some way of being, you just can't see yourself as anything different. Or did you lose a job, a client, a friend, or a relationship and can't seem to be complete or healed?

It is in surrendering and releasing control that you will attract what you REALLY want.

When you lose a dream, you often find your destiny.

And it just might be that your loss of that relationship, client, job, friend, or opportunity **had to happen** for you to come to a place where you could finally surrender control and be open to a greater possibility.

Make no mistake—I am not condoning divorce. I believe in marriage and what it brings to two people who choose to be together. But when the two people grow apart, have different goals, and cease to support each other, they've got to stop, evaluate the situation, and make a choice to either recommit or accept that it is in everyone's best interest to evolve the marriage into a new relationship.

*It's all about accepting what is and **releasing to receive!***

Read that again. That profound statement will help you make sense of senseless events, build faith, regain courage, and restore your confidence through the toughest of challenges.

The French tutor that I had taught me to repeat, "C'est comme ça," which means "It is what it is." I found great comfort in that mantra. You will discover a tremendous peace in your life, too, when you come to the place of simply accepting what is.

Watch yourself. When you start to put a meaning to situations in your life, you lose your power. For example, if you applied for a job and didn't get it, it doesn't mean you won't get another job. It doesn't mean you're a bad person. It doesn't mean the boss hiring for the position was an idiot.

It just means: You didn't get the job. Period.

Don't exhaust yourself by placing any other meaning to it. Use the "C'est comme ça" mantra and let it help you accept what is as just what is.

Does that make sense?

You create so much unnecessary pain in your life when you attach meaning to everything that happens to you!

*The pain that you create now is always some form of unacceptance, some form of unconscious resistance to **what is!***

If you are having difficulty to accepting what is, consider this: It's possible that you are in denial to what you really want.

Let me explain...

I believe that everything I have in my life, whether it's labeled "good" or "bad," I have chosen. Do you?

When I took responsibility that I am the cause for everything in my life, things began to change!

You Are the Cause for Everything in Your Life...

When Mark first moved out, I became aware at how much silent pain I had been living in while still in the marriage. I had gotten used to the pressure and began to think of it as "normal."

I was also lazy and didn't want to make the effort that counseling would entail. I had a fear of failure and didn't want to admit to my family and myself that this marriage wasn't working.

So I did the most dangerous thing a woman can do: **I lived in denial.**

It's like when you're a "little overweight" and you get used to your new size and you begin telling yourself that you're comfortable with a few extra pounds.

It's a lie!

You are fat, and you have a choice: Stay that way or lose the extra weight. Period!

What about if you're overworked? You say to yourself, "The job isn't too bad. I can handle it." And then you actually start to believe your own lie. And, if you don't find the courage to tell the truth and you stay in denial, it will lead you to manifest an illness so your body can finally get the rest it needs!

As to your marriage, if it begins to go sour and you move into denial, telling yourself, "It's not that bad," and you never seek help, you are walking on the path of divorce.

You are causing it all...

Most people don't want to tell the truth that they are fat, don't like their job, are overworked, or unfulfilled in their marriage. They think it means they failed. No! Don't let that lie exist in you, Princess. *You only fail if you continue to live in denial and don't take initiative to effect change.*

Be the Cause for Your Deliciously Fun Marriage and Healthy, Happy Family!

Be the Cause for Your Thriving, "Kick-Ass" Business!

Be the Cause for Your Outrageous, Faith-Filled Life!

You are the cause for everything in your life. Know that and start telling the truth...about everything! Give yourself permission to be self-expressed. Don't settle for a mediocre marriage, body, career, friendship, or life. You are a Princess! You have royal blood flowing through your veins. Live like you really believe that!

Anything...Anything...Anything is possible when you accept the truth that you are the cause of everything in your life!

Breakthrough the Payoff in Pain

All this conversation begs the question, "So, if we are the cause for everything in our life, why would anyone continue to live in pain?"

The answer is quite surprising. Most people continue to live in pain—and even create situations to cause them pain—because a payoff comes with it. And they actually become addicted to the pain!

I met a lady at a luncheon one afternoon who spent nearly the entire lunch hour telling us about all the drama in her life. At the end of her stories, she said, "My life is a soap opera, and I am the star!"

What a revealing comment! She was the star all right; the Star of Drama! She had an innate need for excitement and a need for attention. This combination caused her to manifest all these problems in her life to meet this need in an unhealthy way. And attracting all that drama met that need and she was now addicted to the drama.

What about you? Has the need for excitement caused you to create problems in your life? Has the drama in your life become a habit and now you find your identity in your dramas and problems?

It's insane behavior! But most people have created a victim mentality in some areas of their life. And now it has become a habit. If you have the belief that you are a victim, you will manifest situations that affirm you are a victim.

Consider this…

Are You a Victim or a Victor?

It has been three years since the divorce. Even though I know the incredible power that comes from being the cause of my life, I notice how easy it is for me to go into victim mode.

Without any effort at all, my mind can begin chattering nonsense like "Poor me" or "How am I going to do this by myself?" or "Raising three teenagers is too hard."

I don't even know why these thoughts still come up. Since the divorce, I have a healthier relationship with Mark and our three children than ever before.

I have launched the most successful entrepreneurial venture of my career history. I've taken my kids on a cruise, rented an apartment with them on the Champs Elysees in Paris for the summer, vacationed in Hawaii—four times!—purchased three investment homes, enjoyed countless fun trips with Hans Peter, the most amazing man I've ever met, and experienced a powerful and intimate relationship with my Creator.

I've never been more alive and fully self-expressed in my entire life. Yet, these ridiculous lies can still creep into my mind!

What do you do when the annoying voice of limitation begins to blather? Do you have a discipline in place to silence those voices?

Let me share some simple techniques that I use and teach my coaching clients. It will work for you too.

Silence the Voice of Limitations

First, when you hear the voice of limitation, identify the voice.

Ask yourself, "Whose voice is that?" and name the person. Is it a parent, a teacher, an old friend?

Second, don't ignore the voice. Take a leadership position and reply to the ignorant voice and educate it with the truth. When the voice of limitation speaks, simply reply, "Thanks for sharing; now let me tell you what who I am and what I'm up to."

Educate the voice of limitation. The voice of limitation is just your ego, which you have given power to speak!

Confirm what is working in your business—in your life. Focus on that.

Remind yourself what is working in your life and what you are so grateful for. YOU create the space of gratitude! And gratitude gives you power. It puts you in a space to attract even more great things to you!

What is currently working in your life? Make a list of everything you are grateful for:

_____

_____

_____

_____

_____

_____

Finally, visualize yourself as the victor, not a victim.

Speak to yourself as the victor you are. Confirm it, own it, and focus on you as the victor.

You'd never go to a bad movie twice. Right? So don't allow yourself to watch the movie of limitation. When the picture comes into your mind of you as the failure or of you in limitation, press the stop button of your mind, pull out that stupid movie and put in one that serves you!

Do you see yourself as a victim or a victor?

A person with victim mentality will have a negative attitude about life. They think others are out to get them; true love doesn't exist, life is hard, and building a business is a struggle. These people will inevitably attract negative circumstances to affirm their belief!

The opposite is true as well. People who see themselves as a victor will resonate at a higher energy level, and with that powerful energy they will attract positive things, opportunity, and people. Victors know their circumstance do not have to affect their attitude. They release control of their results and know that all things happen in perfect timing and for their highest good. They have strong faith—faith in themselves, in their ability, in others, and in their Creator, a God who is desperately in love with them!

I've been reading up about the discipline of Tantra. I remember studying it in college, but that's when I held the belief it was wrong, so of course, I learned nothing. (Isn't that interesting?) One of the topics taught in Tantra Sex is

Namaste. Namaste is simply looking at your lover and honoring the light in him or her. Think about what your world would look like if you took this practice and brought it into your business.

Before entering a time of prospecting, you could make a conscious decision to acknowledge the light in that person. When you discipline yourself to see the leader in others, you will inevitably find what you're seeking. When you make a conscious decision to acknowledge the leader, the love, the power in every person, you will inevitably find it.

Wow! What a beautiful reality!

What would our world look like if every person reading this book would make a commitment to BE this type of person? What would your business look like in one year if you committed to practicing this discipline? What would relationships look like if every person practiced Namaste for themselves as well as others?

Take this approach to a higher level and you will be able to see that when a prospect says no to your opportunity, they are NOT rejecting you. They are freeing you from any future frustration that comes from coaxing, manipulating, and prodding a business associate to work their business. It's the same principle with building friendships, dating, or attracting your soul mate!

Make a decision today that you want to sponsor Real Leaders, you want Real Friendships, and you want Real Love in your life. Then, whether you are dating, prospecting, or lunching with friends, your conversations will be different, your relationships will be powerful, and, most importantly, just your being will have a more powerful influence!

The Success Cycle

And when you get tired and a feeling of overwhelm begins to set in, accept the fact that success is a cycle. And when you stop fighting or manipulating that cycle, you stop the chaos and finally realize you have all you need to make your business, and your relationships, and your life work.

The following is the Success Cycle I teach my coaching clients that helps them grow their confidence, conquer fear, banish anxiety, and enjoy the ride of Creating an Outrageous, Faith-Filled Life!

Picture a recycling symbol in your mind. This symbol represents your path of success.

You begin the Success Cycle with great enthusiasm. You're motivated and energized. You can't wait to get to work and accomplish your goals. Your efforts are fueled by enthusiasm.

Picture that stage at the top of your revolving success cycle. Then as you move clockwise around the circle, you experience a setback. You experience rejection. You get a no. You say the wrong thing. You get tired. You lose your focus.

What do you do?

If you are a person who understands that success is a cycle, you will use discipline to make one more sales call. Find the good in another. Forgive. Send out a marketing letter. Say you're sorry. And be the Princess you know you are.

Acknowledge what's working. Be in a state of gratitude. See yourself as the victor. Respect yourself and others. These efforts are fueled by discipline. And then (here's the really good part) your efforts, fueled by discipline, will bring you results, which rekindles enthusiasm! Now, you're back at the top of the success cycle. That's the web and flow of business and life. When you let yourself relax in the flow of life, you stop fighting against the current and move with it.

Everything in your life is just as it is. Right now you are whole and complete. Right now you have manifested everything in your life for a reason. You are that powerful! Now, having said that, if you choose to alter some of the things you have in your life, you have the power right now to do that.

You really can have a successful fulfilling career that brings you more money than you'll ever need.

You really can experience a relationship that lights you up and you feel unconditionally loved every day.

You really can have a healthy, fit, sexy body that is full of energy and vitality.

You have all you need to make your life the greatest masterpiece ever created. And it's all inside of you waiting for you to discover it!

In the next Chapter you will gain clarity into what you really want and learn how to manifest it. Through the Power of Attraction, you'll learn how to attract your soul mate, manifest money, find a fulfilling career, and create your Dream Life!

"What the hell—you might be right, you might be wrong... just don't avoid."

—Katharine Hepburn

Chapter 4
How to Apply the Miraculous to Achieving Your Goals

What do you think it takes for a woman to achieve all her goals? Think about that before you answer. What does it really take for a woman to accomplish all she wants? Does it take:

Desire?
Focus?
Hard work?
Persistence?
Skill, talent, or proficiency?

It's evident that all of these qualities contribute to achieving goals. However, all of these actions combined are not as powerful as the one I am about to share with you.

In this chapter I want to teach you one of the most important concepts of the Don't Mess With the Princess! message. It will help you achieve anything and everything you want. The most powerful way to achieve all your goals in life is found in the Law of Attraction.

Tapping Into the Law of Attraction

I knew I wanted to buy a new car, but I was unsure as to which model suited me best. Finally, after months of deliberating, I decided on the Lexus. Then something interesting happened. I began to see the very car I wanted everywhere I went. I'd see a Lexus in the parking lot of the grocery store. I'd just happen to park next to one in the airport. I'd stop at a light and a Lexus would pull up alongside me. Driving up the interstate, I'd see next a Lexus in the next lane.

As soon as I decided on that particular car, had it on my mind, and gave my attention to it, I noticed Lexus after Lexus wherever I went. They seemed to be following me around, like bees to honey. This is the Law of Attraction in action!

The Law of Attraction simply states that whatever we think about we will attract to us. If we are focusing our thoughts and emotions on prosperity, prosperity is what we will attract. In the same, if we are focused on scarcity or lack, we will attract more of the same.

Have you noticed the Law of Attraction working in your life too?

The Law of Attraction states that you will attract into your life–whether wanted or unwanted–whatever you give your energy, focus, and attention to.

You are constantly giving off vibrations of energy when you think and feel. These vibrations can be picked up and received by other people and things!

When you're feeling happy, loving, appreciative, abundant, prosperous, and peaceful, you are giving off positive vibrations. And you will attract more of that.

On the other hand, if you are feeling sad, lonely, worried, angry, or anxious, then you are giving off negative vibrations. And you will attract more of that.

The Law of Attraction is always working. It's consistent. And for most people that's not a good thing, because most people think about what they don't want. Most people's thoughts are focused on what's not working in their life...and consequently they attract more of the same!

When you walk to the mailbox, are you thinking about finding a wonderful letter from your best friend or a big fat check? Or is your mind focusing on all the bills and late notices?

When the phone rings, are you thinking it's your husband or significant other calling to tell you he loves you, or maybe it's your girlfriend inviting you to a party? Or is your mind focusing on the collection agency, pesky telemarketer, or bad news?

You will attract more of what you think about.

Your thoughts become the very thing that instigates your behavior. And it is your behavior—your way of being—that creates everything in your life. All your power comes from how you choose to respond to life.

That's also the good news!

It's good news because you have complete control over your own thoughts and the way you are being. So let's answer the question that I opened this chapter with.

What does it really take for a woman to accomplish all she wants?

Beyond desire, focus, hard work, persistence, skill, talent, and proficiency—what it really takes for you to miraculously achieve your goals is for you to...

BE what you want!

Practice the power of being, and everything you want will come to you like a magnet—nearly effortlessly!

If you want to build a business with leaders, **be** a great leader. If you want to experience a loving relationship, **be** a loving person. If you want to have joy in your life, **be** a joyful person. If you want to attract wealth, **be** generous with your money.

The most powerful force you have comes from being.

You must realize, however, that this approach to accomplishing your goals is opposite to what you've been doing up to this minute. If you are like most women, you habitually accomplish what you want by doing. Massive action is at the root of most women's success. Think of it—our culture is trained to follow this achievement formula:

Do. Have. Be.

You DO a particular action—lots of it. Then you will HAVE the goal you desire and become the person you want to BE. You've been following this form of achievement for years. And while you may have accomplished some of your goals, I would bet you are exhausted and frustrated with the tremendous amount of exertion that comes from doing, doing, doing!

The Power of Being

The study of quantum physics teaches that success is accomplished in the exact opposite way. Consider the following formula:

Be. Do. Have.

Here's the process of attraction in action: You want something. You declare what it is you want, and you BE that person now. And from that being, you'll DO the actions that reflect who that person is, and then you will achieve your goals and HAVE what you desire. Attraction includes the word action. You actions come from your way of being.

Accomplishing your goals begins with BEING.

The Law of Attraction says you will attract whatever you are. Just like a magnet, you are consistently drawing everything in your life toward you. Whether these are people, opportunities, good things or bad things, you are attracting exactly what you are being. And what you are being comes from what you are thinking. Your life already reflects this powerful concept.

Everything you have right now in your life you attracted. The car you drive, the man you're involved with, the friendships you've created, the job you report to, the children you raise, the money you have or don't have—all came to you through the power of attraction. Your thoughts and the way you've been "being" created every thing you have in your life.

Think about what goes through your mind every day. Right now, put this book down and take note of all the thoughts you've had today. Were they thoughts of abundance or lack?

Take notice of your thoughts right now. Write down what you are aware of in this moment:

_____

_____

_____

_____

Consider this...

If you are always thinking about the bills you have to pay or worrying whether you'll have enough, what are you being? You are being scarcity and fear. And just like a magnet...

The only thing you can attract is scarcity and fear!

If you are making prospecting calls and you are thinking about getting rejected or getting a no, you are being negativity and lack.

And the only thing you can attract is negativity and lack.

And finally, if you are always thinking about what your husband, boyfriend, or men in general do wrong or how you have been hurt and disappointed, you are being a victim.

And the only thing you can attract is more of the same!

Do you really get this powerful principle?

You are in control of everything that happens in your life! Whatever you are thinking, you are being. And whatever you are being will attract more of it to you—just like a magnet. That's why it's imperative that you are always working on and developing your best self! *Every business success is preceded by a personal success—a personal growth.*

Read that again.

While this Law of Attraction principle is true with your negative thoughts and being negative, the reverse is also true and just as powerful. If you are being joyful, loving, powerful, and dependable, you will attract joy, love, power, and dependability.

And THAT, Dear Princess, is where you are miraculous! You have the ability to heal this planet, cure ailments, usher in love, cause a phenomenon, restore relationships, and create extraordinary lives for yourself and everyone in your sphere of influence. Just by your powerful being!

As I sat having breakfast the other day, I couldn't help but overhear the conversation between the two women sitting next to me. They were deep into a full-fledged men bashing session! One lady said, "Men are assholes." The other women nodded her head in agreement and added, "It's so hard to find a good man anymore." And then they began to regale story after story to support their beliefs.

How were these women being? They were being hopeless and negative.

What do you think they will inevitably attract to themselves? Even if there are seventy-seven kind, faithful, wonderful, loving men in the restaurant, *it is impossible for them to attract them!* The only type of men they are able to attract are assholes. Period.

What about the woman who wants to build a million-dollar business, but every time she speaks about her product or service to a prospect, she is thinking, "This is hard." Or "I want them to say yes, but they'll probably say no." She is being pessimistic and confused. And she can only attract prospects who are pessimistic and confused.

And the woman who wants to lose weight...thoughts of being fat consume her. She is always thinking about gaining weight and can't even enjoy a lunch with her best girlfriend because every time she puts a bite of food in her mouth she feels guilty! She looks at working out as a reason to stop being fat instead of a reason to be healthy. And she is always focused on what she doesn't want. How is this woman being? She is being dissatisfied and unhealthy, which is the very thing she thinks she is changing with her dieting. And she can only attract more dissatisfaction and lack of health. And it's the same with you...

Everything in your life right now you have attracted with the thoughts you hold and the way you are being.

I hope you really get this. You have so much power, Dear Princess! Your thoughts and who you are being create your life. Whether it's relationships, business, or health, you create your life with your thoughts.

I know I have repeated this truth a lot in this chapter. But I am committed to your grasping this concept because I know the impact your life will have on the planet. It is no accident that you are reading this book. It is by Divine Order that you picked up this book. You have been chosen for great things. I know the impact you will have when you grasp and live out this powerful truth...

- You will heal yourself and the people in your life.
- You will have the power to usher in love for yourself and others.
- You will attract wealth and abundance for yourself and every person who is in your sphere of influence.

Who you are being makes a difference for everyone! Do you really get that? When you choose to give up and sit in front of the television set, it affects the women across the globe. When you choose to be angry or withhold love for your husband or children, everyone loses! When you choose to think small and build a little business, that decision has an impact on everyone around you.

You make a difference!

So, are you ready to do some amazing exercises to help you shift your negative thoughts and limiting ways of being? All right then! Let's begin manifesting everything you want in your life...

Before we get into the actual exercises, I want you to grasp fully how powerful you are by understanding what manifesting really is...

Harness the Power of Manifesting

I have spent a lot of time researching and discerning the power of manifesting, only to realize I haven't even touched the depths of its power! This fascinating and intriguing search began for me one day while I was reading the Bible.

In the very first book of Scripture, it says, "In the beginning God created..."

In succeeding books of Scripture I don't read the word "create" again. In following Scriptures, it says "manifest" instead of "create."

This got me thinking and questioning. Could it be that ALL things are already created? Everything already exists? And if all things exist right now in this moment, how do they come into existence on this physical plane? How do they become evident, clear, and visible?

Then I looked at the word "manifest." Its very definition is "to be evident, clear, and visible." The first part of that word is "man," meaning "mankind." The other portion of the word is "fest," from the word "festival," which means "celebration"—one of the names for God.

Manifesting is partnering with God. When you manifest you are a vessel, bringing what's already created into the physical plane. You are birthing ideas, people, material things, and love. You are not creating them, for they are already created and exist in the Mind of God. But you are making them evident, clear, and visible.

You are manifesting (Man)i(Fest)ing!

Wow! What a privilege! And what if God, in His infinite wisdom, power, and love, is searching the world for someone who believes she can partner with Him and bring ideas, material things, people, and love to the physical?

Is that woman you?

Most women are afraid of that power. They live a life of busyness and aimless distraction so they won't ever have to come into their true brilliance.

Maybe it's time for you to be different. If you are like me, you are open to exploring the richness of manifesting and partnering with God.

The first step to partnering with God is to become single-minded.

Do Less to Do More

You've simply got to stop doing so much! When you are doing, doing, doing, you are in opposition to manifesting. Isn't it crazy how society, our beliefs, and the example we saw in our own moms taught us that one of the keys to success was multitasking?

It was a lie!

I bought into the whole philosophy of doing ten things at once. Cram another load of laundry in the dryer while I answer the phone, listen to my son while he tells me about his day, write a marketing letter in my head, wonder if I turned off the coffee pot, shoot up a quick prayer, think about what I'm making for dinner, all while I'm visualizing my dream life!

Ha! It was insanity. And it had to stop.

Does your life look like a gyroscope, spinning around at a frantic pace but not going in any specific direction?

Busyness is the enemy that keeps you from harnessing the power of manifesting.

Think of it scientifically. We all know that diffused light has little power or impact, but you can concentrate its energy by focusing it. With a magnifying glass, the rays of the sun can be focused to set grass on fire. When light is focused as a laser beam, it can cut through steel.

That's the power of focused energy.

Now, apply this principle of focused energy to your life. Diffused energy (busyness and aimless distractions) has little power or impact. But when you concentrate your energy by focusing it, you have created a laser beam of power.

What would your life look like next week if you used the power of your attention on ONE project today? That sales letter would be written and sent out. That prospect would have all he or she needs to make an educated decision. That spouse and those kids would feel they are really loved. That closet, garage, office would be organized and free of clutter. There's so much power in focused attention and concentrated energy!

To Harness the Power of Manifesting, Do Less

When you have clarity in your life and focused energy, you are a powerful force.

Okay, Powerful Princess, what is resonating within you? What are you thinking and feeling right now? Just be aware of what's going on inside of you. Write it here:

_____

_____

_____

_____

What activity are you willing to delegate or give up?

_____

_____

_____

_____

In which area of your life do you choose to focus single-minded energy?

_____

_____

_____

_____

What is God saying to you right now?

_____

_____

_____

_____

Now that you have more clarity and are willing to create a single-minded focus, let's talk about how to shift the habitual negative attitudes that most women are bound to. If you're like most, you have created a habitual way of being that is rooted in worry, fear, and negativity. I hope I have made it profoundly clear that you will never attract what you really want until you break the habit of limiting thoughts.

The best way to break the habit of negativity is to ACT in the opposite way of that negative behavior. Act until this "acting" becomes "being". If your habit of behavior is worry, begin acting like you are full of faith. If your habit of behavior is anger, begin acting like you are kind. If you are ill, begin acting like you are healthy. My sister Renee showed me this truth when she dealt with cancer.

How to "Act" Yourself Into Health, Wealth, and Wisdom

"I've just been diagnosed with cancer and I'm going in for surgery," my sister Renee calmly said.

My mind went blank. I clutched the phone, took a breath, and tried to speak. But before I could say a word, Renee began telling me survivor stories—stories about women who beat cancer by choosing to be a survivor and then acting like one. She finished her narration with her intent to implement in her own life the way of "being" found in all of the survivors she researched. She would be healthy by making healthy food choices, following her doctor's orders, and visualizing her cells as vital and healthy.

Today, Renee is completely cancer-free. She has become one of those survivors whom she studied and learned from. *I believe Renee became a survivor the day she decided to BE a survivor and ACT like one.*

It's the same for you and me. We become an entrepreneur when we decide to ACT like one. We become a multimillionaire when we begin to ACT like one. We become a happily married person when we ACT like one. We become a great mom or dad when we begin to ACT like one!

I read an article in *Psychology Today* that reported a study done about human behavior and success. While the article spoke about the importance of positive affirmations and thought, this was not what made the greatest difference in the people studied.

The people in the study who experienced the greatest—and most rapid—success were the people who changed the way they behaved. In other words, they "acted out" the results they wanted. The conclusion of the study was:

"People don't think their way into positive actions as fast as they ACT their way into positive thinking."

What about you? Do your ACTIONS look like they belong to a person who is healthy, wealthy, and wise? Or do they look like they come from a person who is living a life of mediocrity? You'll stop thinking small when you stop acting small.

Begin acting like you're healthy, rich, and wise, and you will begin attracting opportunity to be healthy, rich, and wise.

Several months ago I went to Nordstrom with my daughter Auriana. After a day of shopping, we walked into the coffee shop where I immediately spied a luscious-looking peanut butter and chocolate dessert. Salivating, I suggested to Auriana that we treat ourselves and split it. When she turned me down, I reluctantly ordered just a cup of coffee.

A few minutes later a gentleman in his late seventies walked over to our table. "I could tell how much you wanted this," he says as he placed the peanut butter and chocolate delicacy in front of me. "Let me treat you today."

That dessert only cost the man a few dollars. But the impact it made on both Auriana and me was profound. We both felt cared for and loved.

Several months later, Auriana and her cousin were shopping at the mall when they decided to have lunch in the food court. When it came time to pay for their order, Auriana pulled out her wallet and announced she wanted to treat her cousin to lunch. Her cousin hugged Auriana and told her how happy that made her feel!

On that same day I happened to be at a convention in New Orleans. As I stood in a long line at Starbucks waiting to order my cappuccino, the lady behind me struck up a conversation. When it is finally my turn to order, I told the guy behind the counter to put this woman's cappuccino on my bill. You would have thought I bought her a convertible Maserati!

You know what? That cappuccino cost me only three dollars and fifty cents. The lunch cost Auriana just six dollars. The dessert cost the older gentleman a couple of bucks. What a small price to pay for the rich feeling that these actions produce.

Are your actions rich?

You'll begin thinking big when you start acting big. And when you think love, generosity, and power, you begin being love, generosity, and power.

To Harness the Power of Manifesting, Act Yourself Into a New Way of Being

You shift your way of being by "acting" the way you want to be. You will become courageous when you begin acting courageous. You become loving when you begin acting loving. You act the way you want to be until it becomes a second nature to you.

Be aware of what's going on inside you and write what you're thinking and feeling. Write what you notice here:

_____

_____

_____

_____

_____

What specific negative action are you willing to give up? What new way are you ready to begin acting?

_____

_____

_____

_____

In which area of your life do you choose to raise your standard of being?

_____

_____

_____

_____

What is God saying to you right now?

_____

_____

_____

_____

You're doing it, Princess! You are shifting the planet right now through your willingness to shift yourself! I am so proud of you and celebrate the power that you and I have to heal, love, and manifest abundance!

Applying the "Be. Do. Have." Principle

Now let's get real specific and talk about how to apply the "Be. Do. Have." Principle to your life so you begin attracting all you need to achieve what you really want.

80

Here are the basic steps to the process:

Step One: Choose a specific area in which you want to achieve success and create an intention for that success.

Step Two: Make a list of behaviors you believe exemplify this intention.

Step Three: Be fiercely committed to being these behaviors.

Now let's personalize it for you. In Step One, you state what your goal is. Some examples are:

I want to be the owner of my own business and make millions of dollars.

I want to be a healthy, fit, vivacious woman who lives life with energy and vitality.

I want to be a philanthropist and give millions of dollars to charity.

I want to be happily married and enjoy living life to the fullest with my husband.

I want to be an influential mom and raise healthy, happy kids.

Now it's your turn.

Step One: Choose an area you want to achieve success in. State your intention.

_____

_____

_____

_____

In **Step Two** you identify the behaviors (the way of being) achieving this goal incorporates. Ask yourself:

What are the behaviors of a multimillion dollar female entrepreneur? How does she greet people? Introduce herself? Treat her spouse or children? How does she dress? Carry herself? Give interviews? Treat her employees, clients, and staff?

What are the behaviors of a healthy woman? How often does she work out? What are her eating habits? How many desserts, snacks, alcoholic drinks, or other "empty calories" does a healthy woman eat a day? How much time does she spend in meditation, prayer, or alone?

What are the behaviors of a philanthropist? How much money does she tithe and give back? How often does she volunteer her time in a month? When does she get involved in charity? Does she begin her own charity or just support others?

What are the behaviors of a happily married woman? Does she have a "date night?" and if so, how many times a week does she go out with her husband? What are her daily habits for creating intimacy? How are her communication skills? Does she have a therapist or a coach? How much time does she spend apart from her husband? How often do she and her husband pray together?

What are the behaviors of a great mom? How does she communicate to her children? What is her system for discipline? How much time does she spend just being with her children every day? How does she communicate her love to her children when she is away from them?

Here's the fascinating part...

It doesn't matter if the behaviors you think happy, healthy, and wealthy women have are true or not. It only matters that they are aligned with your beliefs and values and that you follow through with being these qualities. When you begin implementing these actions something triggers in your subconscious. You actually begin believing you are these qualities. And when you believe you are happy, healthy, and wealthy, you will attract the opportunities and people to support it.

Create your list of behaviors of a healthy, wealthy, and wise woman below. Answer the question "How are they "being"?:

The behaviors of a millionaire business woman are:

_____

_____

_____

_____

The behaviors of a healthy, fit woman are:

_____

_____

_____

_____

The behaviors of a female philanthropist are:

_____

_____

_____

_____

The behaviors of a happily married woman are:

_____

_____

_____

_____

The behaviors of a wonderful mom are:

_____

_____

_____

_____

In **Step Three** you choose to be fiercely committed to being these characteristics. Act them out in your behaviors until they become who you are! Be relentless to your commitment. And when you don't feel like being one of the characteristics, focus on your commitment more than your feelings.

What specific behaviors will you begin implementing in your life right now? Make a commitment to be your goal right now. Make a list of your new "ways of being":

I make a commitment to behave like a million dollar business owner.
My way of being is:

_____

_____

_____

_____

I make a commitment to behave like a healthy and fit woman.
My way of being is:

_____

_____

_____

_____

I make a commitment to behave like a philanthropist.
My way of being is:

_____

_____

_____

_____

I make a commitment to behave like a happily married woman.
My way of being is:

_____

_____

_____

_____

I make a commitment to behave like a wonderful and inspiring mom.
My way of being is:

_____

_____

_____

_____

Wow! That is so powerful, dear Princess! The world is being shook up, and you are the cause of this earthquake, this shift in the world! You are making a difference. Who you are creates a tremendous impact on the world. When you implement these behaviors in your everyday life, you have the most powerful force working for you to help you create success. And that powerful force is the force of "being."

And remember, sweet Princess, when you get tired and want to quit being your commitment, think of me. Every word I write in this book I am living. So I know what you're going through. I recognize it can get tough. I realize you may feel like reverting to your old ways. But don't!

Please know that I am praying for you and I ask God to pour out His supernatural strength over you and over me. We are connected in the invisible, and I believe we will meet one day and realize that connection. Who we are makes a difference. So stand strong, Princess. Be loyal to your commitments more than to your feelings. And know that I stand right next to you, visualizing this incredible transformation of the planet by being the very things we want to transform!

Be love.

Be joy.

Be wealth.

Be peace.

Be health.

Be abundance.

Be happiness.

Be a Princess!

In the next chapter we'll move into the really fun part of manifesting. Let's talk about you when you were five years old...

"You may be disappointed if
you fail, but you are doomed if
you don't try."

—Beverly Sills

Chapter 5

Practice Extravagant Dreaming!

Picture this...

A little girl is crawling around a new surrounding when she notices, for the first time, a huge staircase. As the little girl gazes up at the new apparatus, what thoughts do you think are going on in her mind?

Does she say to herself, "Wow! Look at those stairs. Let me at 'em! I'm going up!"

Or does, does she look up at those stairs and think:

"Wow I've got to get to the top! But, wait a minute... I didn't go to stair climbing school. Maybe I'm not ready. I'll just wait until I have my degree in stair climbing, and then watch me go!"

Or

"Wow, I've got to get to the top... But wait. I might get hurt. I may fail. I've heard it said 22 percent of one-year-olds fall on staircases. In fact, CNN just announced stair climbing as a code orange! It's too risky."

Or even

"Wow, I've got to get to the top... But wait. What will my friends say? What if I succeed? They may think that I don't fit in with the group back in the sandbox. They might think I'm one of those snobby, famous stair climbers. You know what they say... It's lonely at the top. I better not. It's just too risky."

NO! A little girl wouldn't say any of these things, for she is hungry for adventure! Children have an inborn, risk-taking ability. It is their nature to risk! They see it. They want it. They take it.

Now, what you need to understand is you know this little girl—because this little girl is YOU! You were once one year old. You once had incredible risk-taking ability. You used to see it, want it, take it.

So, what happened? What happened to that empowering risk-taking ability that you were born with?

Life happened. Circumstances evolved. Disappointments occurred. And you, like me, began to let fear creep in. Slowly and surely, fear began to grow until it was bigger than your dream, bigger than your faith.

You can break through this negative behavior of living by making a conscious effort to become more childlike—not childish—but, childlike.

Cultivate Your Child-Like Thinking

One of the first habits you can incorporate to rekindle the risk-taker and big dreamer in you is to cultivate your child-like thinking. When was the last time you tapped into your imagination and spent a day, a weekend—or a whole week dreaming about the possibilities for you in your life? When was the last time you spent time alone thinking about what you really want and how you can manifest it?

Find amazement with the little things in life things again!

Did you know that a butterfly's life span is two days—and that they are never babies? They go right from the cocoon to an adult butterfly?

Did you know the more pollution in the air, the more bold and brilliant the sunsets?

Did you know that baby zebras recognize their mommies by the positioning of their stripes—and the stripe patterns are never duplicated!

Isn't it amazing that alligators lay their eggs at different levels in the ground. And this action determines the gender of the newborn alligator?

Isn't it amazing that it is impossible to be mad and laugh at the same time? Isn't it amazing that you can cause a grown man or woman with a tough exterior to melt like butter when you say, "I love you."

Isn't it amazing that young children who just meet each other can play like they are lifelong friends within a few seconds?

These seemingly insignificant facts can cause you to wake up. Wake up and think differently. Wake up and notice the abundance of wisdom, love, and miracles that are found in life! Wake up to opportunity that is there for you—waiting for you to notice and respond.

Just imagine what your life would look like if you called on your natural risk-taking ability. Imagine what your business would look like if you cultivated your childlike thinking. Imagine what your relationships would look like if you were willing to really love!

Allow your mind to think extravagantly and you will begin to dream extravagantly! You know—the kind of dreaming you did when you were a kid. Your dreams were so big, you knew you had to grow into them.

It Is Your Nature to Dream Big!

It may take courage to dream big. But the reality is, it is your very nature to do so. Think of it, we are the only creatures in all of creation with the ability to dream! You are made in the image of God. The ultimate Creator! So, of course you were born to dream God-sized dreams.

That's the important point I want you to realize here. When you don't allow yourself to dream big, you are "out of your nature." If you allow yourself to stay in that unfulfilling, unnatural place for too long, you run the risk of producing a scarcity pattern—a limiting consciousness. This is so unnatural for you!

A lack mentality is abnormal. That's why you are so unhappy. You are out of your natural state when you think lack and limitation. And you are the only person who can break yourself free of this limiting consciousness and reclaim your natural state of abundance.

Do you believe that anything… anything… Anything Is Possible?

You used to believe this. Could it be that a collection of unfulfilled dreams has caused you to lose this precious gift? You can rekindle your innate, God-given consciousness of abundance by letting yourself think and dream extravagantly again.

Anything Is Possible!

Did you know that NASA, with all of its super computers and billion-dollar budget, cannot duplicate the flight pattern of a dragonfly or a bumble bee? Aerodynamically, neither the dragonfly nor the bumble bee should be able to fly. Yet, just today I have seen dozens of them fly around my backyard.

The dragonfly and the bumble bee defy logic.

When was the last time you defied logic? When was the last time something happened in your life that you cannot explain and was beyond your human ability?

I was looking through my gratitude journal the other day and was shocked to notice that most of the really great things that have happened in my life had very little to do with my control or my power. The really BIG, outrageous dreams that came true seemed to happen beyond my efforts—in fact, often in spite them!

I don't admit this to suggest that we might as well all take it easy or to imply our lives are predestined no matter what we do. I bring it up to remind you to think about your beliefs of the miraculous and the unexplainable. Do you believe these kinds of things happen to someone like you?

In the book The Ideas of the Great Philosophers, author William Sahakian explains the many views and thoughts on logic and truth. It's interesting to realize that all of the great philosophers agree that scientific truths are often beyond the scope of the human mind and our five senses.

X-rays, light waves, chemical reactions, and a host of other natural phenomena cannot be sensed, though they are understood and demonstrably real.

Think about your five senses and how limiting they can be. A straight stick placed in water appears bent to our sense of vision. We know a mirage is not real, but it looks that way to our eyes. Sounds with a wave frequency above 20,000 cycles per second are not detected by our auditory sense, yet they are detected indirectly. Six pencil points touching a person's back are sensed as only one point.

There are countless human experiences that cannot be seen, proven, or measured on a scale, yet they are undeniably real. One of these realities is love. Love can not be seen. But it can be felt and experienced. The wind cannot be seen. But, like love, it is felt and we notice its effects. Intuition can not be identified or measured on a scale, yet we have all experienced a gut feeling.

Our logical mind and human senses are limited!

Now, before you hyperventilate... know that I believe the logical mind is powerful, and it is important to develop it, consult it, and allow it to direct you. Logic will help you analyze and discern.

However, this same power can cause you to miss out on opportunity and keep you from living life to the fullest! Some people spend great effort developing their mind and then their mind will not allow their Spirit to rule—or to even be heard.

Wisdom is the combination of the mind and the Spirit.

One without the other is misleading, limiting, and even dangerous. Logic without intuition creates robots and limits possibilities. Intuition without logic creates ambiguity and confusion.

You have both of these gifts inside of you. When you couple your mind power with your Spirit (your intuition, gut feelings, and faith) you have created the most effective and powerful force in existence!

For me, the Bible holds countless biographies of people who know how to use wisdom to experience the supernatural fulfill the really profound. Reading these testimonies has helped me realize it's real and notice the miraculous even in today's world.

Now, granted your dream may not be revealed to you in a burning bush or an explicit dream, by an angel or an apparition appearing before you, but God is still in the business of placing BIG dreams in the heart of his people.

What would your life look like if you were to dream outside your own human potential?

Okay, Magnificent Princess: What is resonating within you right now? Be aware of what's going on inside you and what you're thinking and feeling. Write what you notice here:

_____

_____

_____

_____

If you really believed anything is possible, what specific dream would you begin manifesting? World peace? Cures for diseases? Growing a multimillion dollar business? Writing a best-selling book? Being a speaker and a world-changer? Tithing 50 percent of your income? Write your Big Dream here:

_____

_____

_____

_____

What small step toward your dream could you take right now?

_____

_____

_____

What is God saying to you right now?

_____

_____

_____

_____

A Princess has big, bold, and unreasonable dreams

One way to recognize a God-sized dream is by evaluating your reaction to it. If when you think about your BIG dream you get that feeling of intensity in the pit of your stomach, you can be sure, that's the BIG dream God put in your heart even before you were born. Big dreams create a fire in your gut, an intensity in your heart, and a passion in your life that will touch, move, and inspire you to manifest it!

Crafting an Empowering Vision

I want your dream to be so real to you that you can feel it, smell it, see it, and describe it as if you've lived it before! That's what crafting a vision will do for you. It is the fuel you need to resonate at a higher consciousness and attract the people and opportunities you'll need to manifest your Big Dream.

A compelling vision is a thirty-second movie clip that depicts what achieving your big dream will look like. This vision is like a motivational vitamin—available for you whenever you need a shot of energy to get you resonating at a higher consciousness.

Think about the movie industry for a minute...

What does every producer create before their blockbuster movie comes out? If your answer is a trailer, you guessed it. A trailer is a mini-movie that shows the highlights of the film. It helps sell the success of the movie. It entices you enough that you'll reach into your wallet and pull out the ten bucks it costs to go see it. It's actually big business in Hollywood. I have a high school friend who's made millions of dollars creating these much-needed trailers.

Like the movie trailer, your compelling vision will entice you to stay focused on your dream, attract what you need, and give you energy to do what it takes to achieve it.

Now, answer this question... Have you ever walked out of a really bad movie? If you paid your ten bucks and the movie was bad, would you sit through it? No! You'd get up and walk out. And you would never sit through a bad movie twice. Right?

So why do you play a bad movie in your mind over and over? Don't fool yourself. There is incredible power in what you allow your mind to think about. We know this, and yet most of us get stuck playing a "bad movie" over and over again.

You know those movies, the ones where you messed up, lost a sale, got dumped, heard a "no," or didn't make the goal. These negative movie clips drain your energy.

So why do you allow yourself to play them? Stop it! Press the delete button, take out the movie and throw it away! Then, put in a "movie" that fires you up and empowers you.

I know the power that comes from crafting a compelling vision. I used this effective practice to accomplish many of my Big Dreams...

While I share with you the three Big Dreams that I have achieved, I want you to notice how much I have grown in my own consciousness and development. You, too, will grow into bigger and bigger dreams as you grow your faith and get results.

First, I used the power of vision in accomplishing one of my Big Dreams in my direct sales business...

It was the last day of our annual company convention. As I sat in the audience, I dreamed of walking up on stage at the following year's convention and accepting the award for top recruiter. And I set the goal that day. However, the dream I had and the goal I set was not enough to achieve Court of Recruiting for the following year. The dream and the goal was only the first step.

This is what I did next...

After everyone had left the convention hall, I sneaked backstage. I walked out on the platform and looked out at the 10,000 empty seats, closed my eyes, and began creating my vision of success:

I'm standing tall in a glittering royal blue gown. I smell the intense fragrance from the botanical garden that surrounds the stage. I hear my name echoing over the sound system and begin walking—no, gliding—down the fifteen steps (I counted them!) I accept my diamond ring and the keys to my brand new, shiny car. I feel the overwhelming love from all of my team members in the audience as they look up at me. We share a warm smile and celebrate success together!

What do you think was the first thing I did when I returned from that year's convention? The first thing I did was I bought the dress! I found a glittering royal blue gown and hung it outside my closet so I could see it everyday. I began playing that powerful thirty-second movie clip in my mind over and over again. I created an emotional attachment to my goal and began to really believe I could achieve it. I raised my consciousness and began attracting the people and opportunities that helped make my dream come true.

When the overwhelming amount of sales and recruiting calls got me down and the phone began to feel like a 3000-pound rock, I'd stop what I was doing and play my movie clip. Instantly I reconnected with my desire of that dream and couldn't wait to pick up the phone and share my business opportunity and help someone else achieve their dreams!

That's the power of crafting a vision.

The next year's convention was the opportunity to live out that vision I had played thousands of times in my mind, with a few surprises...

I felt like royalty when I heard my name bellowing through the auditorium: "Lisa Jimenez, Court of Recruiting!" I stepped on stage in my royal blue gown—that I had to take out a size because I was five months pregnant! (Ha, I guess when you're so focused on your dream, you forget to take your birth control! It was a thrill to accomplish that dream with Connor, my third-born child.)

I glided down the fifteen stairs and had to catch myself a few times, so stunned was I at having a man waiting at every step to take my hand and guide me. This was not in my vision. And that vision had become SO real to me that any alteration to it was surprising. It was wonderful to be standing around the botanical gardens as I received the keys to my new car and my diamond ring.

Dreams really do come true!

Fast forward about five years. I create a goal to host business retreats for entrepreneurs in exotic cities around the world. After I begin sharing my idea with some of my clients, I realize it's time for me to craft another empowering vision.

This time I jump on a plane to Paris, France, for the weekend. I tour the city's most incredible hotels, visit the amazing restaurants, and discover some phenomenal excursions on which I could take my participants. In just three days, I booked the hotel rooms in a phenomenal property right on the Champs Elysees. The reservations for all the excursions and fine dining were made. And I even bought a few of the gifts I would place in the participants' hotel room each night. The most bizarre part of this story is that I didn't have one person signed up for the retreat yet! I just stepped out in faith, knowing that I achieved a big dream once before and I knew how to use the power of vision and attraction to do it again!

Throughout the next several months I kept visualizing this incredible experience. I pictured all the participants sitting around the Mastermind table, sharing ideas for building our businesses. I felt the warmth of the commitment and loved shared between each person as we helped each other manifest our best lives. I smelled the fragrance of the Louvre gardens as we enjoyed the tour through paris on our motorized Segways. I tasted the delicious cuisine as we dined in the famous restaurants. I experienced this phenomenal retreat even before it actually happened!

It was just nine months later that I stepped out of the limousine along with all of the participants of the Rich Life Mastermind Retreat in Paris, France!

Dreams really do come true!

Crafting an empowering vision and watching it every day in your mind helps you make your big dream real before you achieve it. You can taste it, smell it, feel it, and experience your big dream every day on the way to achieving it. And that, my dear Princess, will create the consciousness you need to attract the people and opportunities to make your dream come true.

There's an important point I want you to notice about these two visions. First, the royal blue and silver gown cost me about fifteen hundred dollars and helped me manifest my first big dream. The trip to Paris and reserving the hotel suites cost about fifteen thousand dollars and helped me manifest my second big dream.

Isn't it interesting how much I've grown!? And when you think about it, what's the difference between $1,500 and $15,000 besides just another zero and a lot more belief!

And just to let you in on a little secret...

I am crafting an empowering vision for the *Don't Mess With the Princess!* message. My Big Dream is to be the first author to publish a billion books. I want this powerful message in every woman's life.

I am committed to the transformation of women and relationships. My possibility is "Marriage and Family United in the Spirit of Self-Expression."

And the empowering vision I created and watch every day in my mind is this...

Today is November 11, 2011, (that's my favorite number 11.11.11) and I am so grateful for the amazing life I live! I sit here next to my wonderful husband who is so loving and supportive of me and my message to the world. We are in the front row of the Bastille Theater in Paris, France, next to Beau, Connor, Mark, his new wife, and all of our family and friends, as we smile with anticipation to watch Auriana's opening night!

Auriana just graduated from Yale University and immediately got hired with the London Theater to write and direct a theatrical play. Beau and Connor are so proud of their sister! They are doing great in college and are excited to have such bright futures in front of them.

We just completed our North American tour and shared the Princess message on every major talk show. It was so much fun to be interviewed by Larry King, the *Today* show, *Good Morning America*, *Live with Regis and Kelly*, *The View*, and all the other talk shows. The Princess message is so well-received and continues to make a profound impact on women and the world!

Tomorrow, after we celebrate Auriana's theatrical debut, we begin our international tour. We are scheduled on every major talk show all over Europe, Australia, and Japan. *Don't Mess With the Princess!* has been published in over seventy languages, and we will triple that number by the end of the year.

Every day I receive countless e-mails and cards from women—and men—who have manifested their Big Dreams and are major contributors to healing this planet. The consciousness of the human race has transformed to abundance and love. Marriages are working. Female billionaires are on the rise. Women are in every major leadership position from politics to business. Cures for diseases are being discovered. And people are being healed! There are homes and food for every child. And the world is transforming into a place of harmony and grace!

And I am so very grateful to the living, loving God and to Jesus the Christ who chose me to write this powerful message and empower me every day to keep my commitment of transforming women and the world!

That is my next Big Dream and my empowering vision to manifest it! I am filled with love and gratitude as I write it and feel so very blessed to have the insight, confidence, and support to manifest it!

So, what about you? What is the compelling vision that supports your Big Dream?

Sit back with a cup of coffee or tea and begin writing your vision of achieving your Big Dream. Then, watch this "movie" in your mind every day to help you create the consciousness you'll need to attract the people and opportunities to make your dream a reality.

Craft Your Empowering Vision here:

Today is

_____

My Big Dream is

_____

I am so grateful for

_____

_____

_____

_____

_____

_____

_____

I invite you to e-mail your compelling vision to me at Lisa@ilovetheprincess.com and I will do my best to respond to you and keep your Big Dream in my prayers.

Before you move on to the next chapter, do this assignment. Take the time to declare your Big Dream and write out your Compelling Vision! If you are still not convinced how vital this exercise is, let me say this...

The world needs you to dream outrageous dreams. Think about it. We are living in a theater of the absurd. We have young men who fly planes into buildings and walk into crowded areas with bombs strapped to themselves. We have shows that promote sexual promiscuity—or you'll get voted off the island! We have the unmentionable occurring in our world today. And you have the ability to shift all that, Powerful Princess.

Are you willing to believe, think, and act unreasonably, boldly, and powerfully?

Imagine you had infinite money, infinite time, infinite opportunity, infinite ideas and resources... What would you dare to dream?

What bold, audacious, and miraculous dream will you choose?

Anything is Possible!

Have fun, Creative Princess, with declaring your Big Dream, crafting your Vision, and watching God work in supernatural ways to manifest it with you!

"Security is mostly a superstition. It does not exist in nature. Life is either a daring adventure or nothing."

—Helen Keller

Chapter 6

Powerfully Dealing With Breakdowns, Setbacks, and Disappointments

Okay, let's face it. Sometimes life sucks...

Occasionally, you don't get that big contract or job promotion. From time to time a good friend will hurt your feelings. Every so often you'll lose something that's important to you. Now and again you'll hurt a precious loved one. Friends move away. Plans get cancelled. Bags get lost.

What do you do when things break down and don't go your way?

Society tells us to "grin and bear it." Conventional wisdom says to learn from it. Motivational speakers show us how to move past it. All of this is vital. However, too often women who are faced with a problem or a breakdown handle it in one of two extremes. They deny it or manipulate it.

Let's talk first about denying a breakdown...

If you have ever denied feeling disappointed, pretended something didn't really hurt you, lied about your real feelings, or deprived yourself of any emotion, you are not living as powerfully as you could be.

The Privilege of the Pity Party

When I feel a negative emotion, I let myself feel it—without it owning me or overpowering me. I give myself an hour or less to deal with the disappointment or breakdown. That's usually the time it takes to go for a jog in my neighborhood. I throw on my running shoes and hit the pavement! Sometimes I'm silent and introspective. Other times I'm crying and yelling out to God how hard things are. I know I probably look absolutely ridiculous! But when I'm done with my "Pity Party," I feel so much better! In fact, I actually feel empowered! I gain a new sense of clarity from allowing myself the privilege of feeling and then being complete with the problem or emotion.

But here's the big warning: Be cautious that you don't pull anyone into "being" the emotions—including yourself! It happens too often that you feel an emotion and start to become that emotion. Always keep your emotions separate from your being. And remember, you are not your emotions!

The main point here is a Princess is whole and complete. The process of being whole and complete comes from living a life of integrity that you honor your feelings, disappointments, and breakdowns.

Now, having said that...

Let's talk about shifting your mindset and beliefs about a breakdown. Answer these questions:

Do you see a breakdown as being weak?

Do you view a breakdown as a reason to quit?

Do you believe a breakdown means you failed?

These are lies! Breakdowns are a part of creating a Big Life. The worse thing you can do is be in denial of the breakdown with statements like "It didn't really matter anyway" or "I don't care."

When you allow a space for your negative emotions, unavoidable disappointments, and inevitable pain, you take away their power over you! We label these events as negative and even let them become reasons to quit or feel inadequate. But they are really just emotions, disappointments, and pain. That's it. That's all they are. Stop giving your emotions so much power. Just realize they are going to happen to the person who is creating an amazing life for themselves and others!

What about you?

When you face disappointment, do you give yourself space to get angry, experience the sadness, sense the sorrow, identify the feelings, and be aware of your reaction without judging, labeling, or destroying yourself? Notice I didn't say, "be angry, be sad, or be lonely." "Being" these negative emotions is dangerous because you could begin finding your identity in them. Allowing your self to "feel" an emotion is quite different than "being" that emotion.

Can you distinguish the difference between feeling an emotion and being it?

You are not your emotions! They do not define who you are. Emotions are just waves of feelings that come with the inevitable events of everyday life. If you fall into the trap of being any of these negative emotions, they will consume you.

Don't call your girlfriend or your husband to vent these emotions before you've given yourself the privilege of the pity party. You want to affirm that you are complete with the problem before you share it with anyone. Then, after you have dealt with the emotion, you are complete with it and can share it with others.

How liberating!

You honor yourself when you allow an emotion to be just what it is. And an emotion is just an emotion. That's all. I'll say it again, an emotion does not define you. It doesn't make you who you are. It's just an emotion! When you feel angry, disappointed, sad, or lonely, it doesn't make you "bad." And letting yourself experience these emotions doesn't make you weak.

In fact, emotions are great teachers. They shout hidden messages to help you be successful, powerful, and healthy. Consider this:

The emotion of fear is telling you "It's time to get prepared."

The emotion of loneliness shouts "It's time to connect."

The emotion of anger lets you know "It's time to take care of myself."

The emotion of dissatisfaction means "It's time to appreciate what I have."

The emotion of apathy is saying, "It's time to take a stand."

Dear Princess, if you really want Real Love, a Multimillion Dollar Business, Loving and Supportive Friends, and an Amazing Life that you love, you have got to be okay with breakdowns, disappointments, pain, and all the other emotions that come under this umbrella.

Deal with your breakdown with the thought "Nothing is wrong here. This is just part of being up to something Big!"

Know this: You will have the breakdowns that are worthy of your life and what you're up to! Wow, do you really get that? If you're up to Big Things in life, then you will experience breakdowns. It's just a part of creating success. And there is nothing wrong with you or the breakdown.

My Life Is a Soap Opera and I Am the Star!

I got a call from Jill, a prospective client of mine, who began telling me about all of the challenges and problems of her life. She lamented about her difficulty in business, crisis in relationships, and disasters with her children. In the midst of this monologue of misery, she stopped said,

"My life is a soap opera, and I'm the star!"

Wow! Here she had to suffer through all these irritating problems—yet she was LOVING it! The constant drama in her life gave her a sense of importance, a feeling of being needed, and a lot of attention!

Jill was right. She is the star of her own "show." And so are you! What does your movie look like? And, more importantly, what is the starring role you've given yourself to play? Do you believe you actually get to choose what role you play in life? You do! So, being the director of you life's movie, what roll do you choose to cast yourself in? Spend some time thinking about that question and make a list of the qualities and values that you want to "play". Then, begin honoring these qualities and values by disciplining yourself to "be" them. You will transform how people view you and treat you because you have transformed the way you view you and the way you treat you!

Make a list of the personality qualities that you "cast" yourself in:

_____

_____

_____

_____

_____

_____

Make a list of the values that are most important to you:

_____

_____

_____

_____

Breaking Through Fear, Worry, and Anxiety

Albert Camus, famous French author and philosopher, once applied names to the previous centuries. He named the seventeenth century as "The Century of Math." The eighteenth was "The Century of the physical." The nineteenth was "The Century of Biology." Then, he shocked the public by naming the twentieth century the century of fear.

Along with this bold statement, came that of philosopher and poet, W.H. Auden. He called our time "The Age of Anxiety."

Newspaper columnist Ann Landers was once asked, "Out of all the thousands of letters you receive each month, what problem is most dominate in people's lives?"

"It's fear!" she replied without hesitation. "People live in bondage with their fear. They're afraid of losing their wealth. They're afraid of losing their loved ones. They're afraid of being themselves. They're afraid of growing up and being responsible. They're afraid of life itself!"

What about you? What fear, hidden or known, is affecting your behavior and keeping you from living your dreams?

In my best selling book, Conquer Fear!, I taught how to break through fear and all of its cousins like worry and anxiety. I suggest you read your copy of Conquer Fear! again to master this topic. However, I want to include a short overview in this book to help you break free from the limitations of fear.

All successful people have to learn how to deal with fear. In all the personal coaching clients I work with I heard story after story about how they, too, had to face and deal with their fear. What I began to notice is how similar the stories were! The names would change. The circumstances were different. But the fear was the same—and very real. I came to understand this profound truth:

The difference between mediocre success and a breakthrough success is your willingness to face and deal with your fear.

Fear is just a part of being human. It exists in every person's life. Fear is a part of every success story and is just part of growing. Fear isn't going away! The profound truth is: It's not fear that keeps you from success...

What keeps you from succeeding is your inability to deal with fear.

Three Steps to Conquer Your Fear

The first step in dealing with your fear is to change your beliefs about it. Change the way you think about fear and you change your reaction to it.

Fear can actually be healthy. Think about it. It is fear that gives you the powerful adrenaline rush so that you will have the ability to flee from a situation that is truly unsafe—the same adrenaline rush to fight to win! Yes, fear is a gift, instilled in you to keep you safe and lead you to faith.

Step #1: Change Your Beliefs About Fear

Begin seeing fear as your green light to GO! Let fear be your sign that you are on to something big! It's just a natural part of building a big business, creating a delicious relationship, and being a world-changer.

The next time you feel that fear, befriend it! Know that it's a common feeling encountered by the person who is up to big things. Don't ignore it. Just notice fear and it will move through you without any effect whatsoever. Let yourself become very present and receive the fear without a fight. It's just a part of creating a big life. Change your belief about the fear and you change your reaction to it. Change your reaction to the fear and it loses its power over you.

Step #2: Use Your Intellect to Move Through the Fear

As a child you would react instinctively to fear. This was acceptable behavior for you then. But, over time, you developed habits of behavior that today cause you to react to fear instead of act. You are not a child any more. You have a developed intellect that you can call upon to move through fear.

You react instinctively to fear by running from it, ignoring it, sabotaging your efforts, or quitting the very dream you said you wanted. These habits of behavior are programmed into you. To interrupt these negative behaviors you need to use your intellect and respond intelligently to the fear.

111

Occasionally fear brings a message. The message could be for you to get prepared. If you have a speech to give and you experience a stifling fear, it could be a warning sign for you to take action in preparing more thoroughly. If you feel a lot of fear when doing a project, it could be a sign that you need to ask for help. The fear is a message to you to reach out to others.

Preparation silences fear! Other people's support silences fear!

Call on your intellect to discern whether the fear you are experiencing is more than just the normal part of creating big things. Let your intellect decipher the message fear could be bringing you.

Step #3: Neutralize Fear With Its Opposite

The opposite of fear is faith. You will neutralize fear by focusing on and growing your faith. Is your faith stronger than your fear?

Where faith is dominant fear is silenced. Faith is like a multivitamin on steroids! It is faith that fosters hope, courage, boldness, and conviction. These are all the ingredients you need to conquer fear.

There was an article in *USA Today* that read, "Faith is more important than food." That was the conclusion of a remarkable medical report, which studied the correlation between stress and ulcers. The report cited that ulcers were by-products of anxiety, worry, and fear. It went on to discuss how faith is the most powerful cure for a patient suffering from an ulcer.

Even the medical community recognizes the power of faith. To an ulcer patient writhing in pain, faith is more important than food. But, this truth applies to healthy people as well. It applies to parents doing all they can to raise healthy, happy kids. It applies to spouses trying hard to keep their marriage alive or even keeping it together. Faith applies to professionals working to build their business. The bigger the goal, the bigger need for faith.

What Really Is Faith?

Webster's definition of faith is "belief, trust, or reliance." The Apostle Paul's definition is "Faith is the assurance of things hoped for and the conviction of things not seen." Do you have the assurance of things hoped for, and a strong conviction that you have all you need to make your life work? Well-known author, Max Lucado, explains faith in the following story:

Imagine you are an ice skater participating in a competition. You are in first place with one more round to go. If you perform well, the trophy is yours.

Then, only minutes before your performance, your trainer rushes to you with the thrilling news: "You've already won! The judges tabulated the scores, and the person in second place can't catch you. You are too far ahead."

Upon hearing the news, how will you feel? How will you skate? How about courageously and confidently? You will do your best because the prize is yours!

Live your life like you've already won. Walk into that job interview like you've already got the job. Ask that girl out on a date like she's already said yes. Ask for that sale like you've already made it!

Albert Camus, W.H. Auden, and Ann Landers exposed our fear. Fear exists. You can neutralize it by cultivating your faith. Have an assurance of things hoped for and a conviction of things not seen and you will shift your beliefs about fear, befriend it, and see it as just a part of creating a big life.

How many lies have you told today? If you're like most women, it's a lot! The lies society tells us and the ones we tell ourselves keep us stuck in mediocrity. Do you know how to identify and break-through those lies? That's what we'll be talking about in the next chapter. And that's no lie!

"Courage is the price that life

exacts for granting peace."

—Amelia Earhart

Chapter 7

Breaking Through the Five Biggest Lies Women Have Been Told

Women have been lied to. And the real shocker is we have chosen to believe in these lies. This chapter is about exposing those lies and helping you claim the truth of who you are as a woman and the powerful contribution you make to the planet.

Please know that I didn't write this chapter for you to like me. There may be times throughout this segment that you won't. What I can guarantee is, if you are willing to go through some discomfort (oh, all right, it may be downright painful!), the message in this chapter will slap you in the face while it heals your heart. It will rock your world while it restores your power. And it will shake your beliefs while it empowers your dreams!

One of the most important points for you to realize right now is YOU have chosen to believe in lies that have held you back. And only YOU have the power to change that. Only YOU can realize the truth, embrace your real power and get on with creating a life you really love.

The 5 Biggest Lies Women Have Been Told:

1. You are not enough
2. There is never enough time
3. You can't have it all
4. It has to be perfect
5. It's a man's world

Big Lie #1: You Are Not Enough

I have never met a woman who is completely satisfied with her body, her career, or her life. Every woman I interviewed for this book shared with me what she would change about herself and her life.

Now, of course it's great to want to improve. We all have the desire to grow and progress. That's not what I am talking about here. The issue I want to discuss with you is the profound dissatisfaction that comes from the Not Enough Syndrome. This type of discontent is a hole that can never be filled.

If you could change anything about you, what would it be? Your personality? Your body? Your entire life?!

Whatever you choose to change, I support you and encourage you to go for it. However, I ask you to make sure you choose to change out of a desire for your own healthy evolution and improvement, not out of the Not Enough Syndrome.

Be completely honest with yourself, would you make the changes for yourself—or make them for others? Most women admit their Not Enough Syndrome stems from other people's opinion of them.

Magazines, Movies, and the Media

Here are some of the titles I found on recent magazine covers...
"Ten Tips to Look Thinner!"
"Five Ways to Get A Guy!"
"How to Look Younger for the Over Forty!"
Now I know these magazines think it's their savvy advice that is

selling subscriptions, but, come on! The reason magazines sell with these titles is because it feeds right into the Not Enough Syndrome. It speaks right to your belief that you are only valuable if you look like a super model and act like super woman!

Pick up any woman's magazine and the message is clear: "Obsess over other people's approval of you."

You are buying into this lie by buying these magazines! And that's what is keeping the lie alive.

Where in your life are you in bondage by the Not Enough Syndrome? Do you feel you aren't pretty enough? Rich enough? Smart enough? Thin enough?

What about your career? Do you believe you don't produce enough? Sell enough? Grow enough? Make enough?

What about your spiritual life? Do you think you aren't praying enough? Helping enough? Donating enough? Worshipping enough?

What about your family life? Do you wonder if you are loving enough? Strict enough? Around enough? Doing enough?

Now, please know, I value growth in all of these areas. I work out every day and eat healthy foods. I give my best efforts to my clients and career. I have a specific prayer time and meditation practice. I enjoy raising my children and respect their dad. I tithe 10 percent to my church and have several other ministries and causes to which I donate my time and money. And I am continuously looking for ways to improve in these areas.

But make no mistake... I choose this healthy life style for me. I am fully aware of the importance of keeping my body extremely healthy with the type of speaking and traveling schedule I have. I enjoy inspiring others and being a part of their success. I love God and having a powerful connection with Him. I get a kick out giving money to charities, causes, and especially young entrepreneurs.

I live this way because I choose it—not because I am supposed to or because it brings me approval, attention, or love.

Do you really get that Princess?

I encourage you to value a healthy lifestyle and live in the way that works for you in all areas of life. But do it because you choose to… period!

NOTE: You will have the opportunity to create "Your Best Life" in Chapter Nine where I will take you through a process of choosing specific goals in the most important areas of life… The fun just keeps coming!

When Are You Enough?

The point I really want to make here is, if you're like most women, you are letting other people dictate who you are. And that has got to stop! It's time for you to powerfully choose what you stand for and what is important to you. And when you choose that and create habits in your life to support that choice, you will be able to answer the big question of *"When are you enough?"*

You have the power to break through the Not Enough Syndrome. Start by recognizing when you fall into it. Notice the occasions when you allow other people's opinions of you to dictate how you see yourself.

Make a list of the most recent times when you were overly concerned with other people's opinions of you in the following categories:

Your Body:

_____

_____

_____

_____

Your Career/Work:

_____

_____

_____

_____

Your Spiritual Life:

_____

_____

_____

_____

Your Family Life:

_____

_____

_____

_____

Only *your* opinion counts, Princess! You will have the greatest impact on the world when you are whole and complete within yourself. When you celebrate who you are right now and know that *you are enough right now*, you create the space for expansion and natural evolution that will bring about an even more powerful life and contribution.

Another important point is that when you celebrate who you are right now and you respect your uniqueness, other people will do the same. A Princess is fiercely committed to her self by honoring her uniqueness, desires, and even her quirks.

I know this can be difficult for you. It is for me, too. I often feel like an alien in this world. Everything about me is unconventional. The type of career I have, the kind of relationships I have, the beliefs I hold, my relationship with God and my Savior Jesus the Christ, and the way I live my life is exceedingly different than those of most women!

But what I have noticed since I took a stand for myself and the way I live my life is how supportive other people are toward me! When I thought I would get a judgmental stare, I got a smile. When

I thought I would receive a snide remark, a word of encouragement came. When I thought I would have to deal with rejection, a helping hand was extended.

The world is ready for powerful women! Are you one of them? Are you ready to accept who you are and what your purpose is, and be "sold out" committed to it?

When you have your own opinion, your own beliefs, and your own presence of mind, you bring value to every relationship you have.

Do you really get that?

Stop obsessing over someone else's approval. Just stop it! Be an independent thinker. Stop living someone else's standards. Choose your own standards and live by them. And, if you're already doing this, stop apologizing for it.

Don't Give Yourself Up!

Cindy had been dating Robert for a few months when he began telling her what outfits to wear. She was mildly annoyed, but responded only with a "Thanks for your thoughts."

But one day when Cindy walked into the living room after getting dressed, Robert said, "You're gonna wear that? You'd look so much better if you wore—"

Before he could finish, Cindy smiled and said, "Listen, Mr. Armani, I have my own style that I love. If you want to dress a Barbie doll, we can stop by the toy store on the way to the movies."

Robert got the message. He smiled back at Cindy and said, "Wow, you are incredible."

Cindy is distinctive and she knows it. She doesn't lose herself when she's in a relationship. She knows who she is, likes that person, and never apologizes if she doesn't "fit" someone else's expectation.

Sarah was an artist with exceptional creative talent. After years of working for corporate, she decided to resign and paint full-time. She had complete conviction that she would be able to make a living as an artist. Her family didn't. They loved her very much and didn't want to see her "fail," so they were not supportive of her new career. Sarah didn't quit. She appreciated her family's concerns, but never lost herself in their fears. Today, she is living her dream. She is a successful artist who has the respect and support of her family.

Carrie was an experienced business consultant who was hired to train the sales division of a pharmaceutical company. At first everyone was receptive to Carrie and her ideas. But that started to shift when she began implementing procedures that made each employee more accountable. A few of the more seasoned employees had never had to report their progress or call in figures at the end of the week. Carrie felt the tension from these few and did something very important: She acknowledged it!

She didn't give up on herself or her program, she believed in herself enough to stand by her program and share the benefits of it with conviction. She called a division meeting and, after letting everyone speak their concerns, she continued to teach her system with conviction and enrolled every employee there. It was her conviction that caused the shift in the room. And those few negative employees began to sit up in their chairs with every benefit Carrie shared. By the close of that meeting, every person was on board and supported the "extra work" that was involved to make the new program a success.

Conviction goes beyond belief. It is a power that comes from your knowing that you were born for just such a time as this. You are the manager, trainer, sales rep who was hired for just such a job as this. And no matter what obstacles or setbacks occur, the belief and conviction you have in yourself and your ability will cause others to be touched, moved, and inspired.

Big Lie #2: There Is Never Enough Time

This lie is on the mind of every woman I know. It is the most common excuse for why women can't, shouldn't, or won't start their own business, learn a new language, enjoy a relationship, volunteer, or get their body in shape.

This lie can be very convenient for women who are stuck in fear. They use the excuse of lack of time, when they are really masking a deep fear of success or a fear of commitment.

The truth is there's no such thing as time in eternity! Isn't that an amazing reality? What would your life look like if you lived in a realm that was free of time?

I am actually on a five-day cruise right now as I write this chapter. Because I am traveling alone, I have no one else to take care of or to consider. This makes time irrelevant. For the past several days, time has not existed for me.

I wake up when I finish sleeping, not when an alarm clock goes off. I eat when I'm hungry, not when the clock says to. I have no boss, kids, responsibilities, or schedule to remind me of time. I'm experiencing timelessness for one of the few times in my life. It has been liberating!

The most profound realization I've made is how productive I am. There are no time barriers placed on me to interrupt the flow of writing. The other interesting realization I notice is how little I eat. I think it's "time" that causes us to think we're so hungry.

"It's time to eat!"

"It's time to sleep!"

"It's time to..."

Time controls so much of what we do and who we are.

I know you can't turn off the clock in the world today. However, I mention this story to help you realize how time controls you, your life, and who you are being. It is not meant to be this way.

Time controls you.

And this reality is costing you—a lot! The harassed lifestyle you have created for yourself causes you to miss out on so much opportunity. You are either focused on the past or living in the future. You are not aware of golden opportunities around you, because you are simply not present to them!

Psychologists say 68 percent of people miss out on opportunity simply because they are not awake to it. Did you read that clearly?

They are not awake. Most people are in a coma of routine, habit, and schedule. They almost have to be. Do you overstimulate your calendar with so many tasks? When you do, you are actually repelling success. An overly busy life creates robots. It becomes necessary to be in a robotic state of "doing" to ensure everything on the to-do list will get accomplished. This kills creativity, possibility, and serendipity!

Caroline was a coaching client of mine who hired me to help her grow her direct sales business. In the primary interview I asked her what she thought was holding her back from reaching her financial goals.

"It's time," she quickly answered. "I just don't have the time to devote to my business with my other responsibilities." Caroline was the mother of two boys, a wife, and very involved with her church.

First I helped Caroline change her belief about time. I knew if she could embrace the belief that there is always enough time, she would naturally begin prioritizing and delegating her tasks which would create more time.

After Caroline became aware of how time was controlling her and made some changes to alter that, we did the next exercise. I wanted to help Caroline shift her view of time from being "the enemy" to being "her friend." Too often we see time as this big, ugly rival whom we have to beat.

Beat the clock...is a common mindset. Quit giving time so much power! Begin viewing time as simply a structure to help you compartmentalize your life.

I gave Caroline an interesting exercise. First, I had her create a mantra to change her belief about time. She began repeating the following: *"God, in His infinite wisdom, made twenty-four hours enough time."*

This helped Caroline to really believe that there is enough time.

Next, I had Caroline chart her day and write down how she spends her time.

A week later I received a phone call from Caroline. She was astounded with the results. She was less stressed and more productive. She felt more fulfilled and happy and had accomplished more that week than ever before.

What is your mantra to help you shift your beliefs about time? Write it here:

_____

_____

_____

_____

What is your relationship with time? Do you need to change it? What can you do to shift it today?

_____

_____

_____

_____

Evaluate how you allot your time. Be empowered to make some much-needed changes in your beliefs about time and your relationship to it.

The final aspect I want to help you shift in your relationship with time is your how it creates a lack of patience. When you rush things to happen, instead of surrendering, you create tremendous stress. Women are notorious for their impatience when it comes to achieving goals, finding their soul mate, or completing a project.

I understand how important deadlines are. I believe in setting goals with due dates. That's why I am on this cruise by myself writing the concluding chapters of this book! Nevertheless, don't be so attached to your deadline that you don't allow the Divine Order to take over and guide you in the best plan and ultimate timing for your goal.

I experienced this phenomenon several years ago when writing my best-selling book, *Conquer Fear!* I was seven months behind and frustrated that I had missed the dead line. What I didn't realize at the time was God had a better plan...the book debuted one week before the tragic event of 911. God is sovereign!

What about you?

Do you believe you have a living, loving Father who is divinely guiding your life? And that guidance includes the timing of when things are best to occur. Don't hold on too tightly to "your plan" or "your deadline." Let serendipity of the Divine Plan lead you and your project. Whether your desire is to find your soul mate, accomplish a goal, or complete a project...

Know that your dreams and your goals will be accomplished in "perfect timing."

One of my favorite mantras is *"It's already on the calendar!"* I repeat this to myself and to my clients whenever we start to get frustrated with the speed of our accomplishments. You can rest in the truth that your life is being led by Divine Guidance and everything you desire has already been created in the future. Your goal will manifest itself in perfect timing.

Relax in the truth that there is always enough time, dear Princess. Maintain your confident posture. Know you are divinely guided and the accomplishment of your goal is already "on the calendar"!

Big Lie #3: You Can't Have It All

I used to believe that it was ungodly and unspiritual to desire too many things. I believed I couldn't have a wonderful marriage AND a successful career. I couldn't have happy, healthy children AND a fulfilling personal life...

And my life reflected these beliefs.

Then one day I was studying the definitions of words found in Scripture. When I researched the word desire, I was amazed to find out what it means. Desire actually means *"of the Father."*

I began shifting my beliefs about what was possible for me, my family, and the world. I had fought myself for so long. I made my husband wrong. I used my children as an excuse for not growing my business. And the amazing part of all this is I thought I was being spiritual!

None of these limiting behaviors were noble. They were all based in fear. I was afraid of success. And I didn't feel worthy of "having it all."

You can read the story of my powerful breakthrough in my best seller, *Conquer Fear!* The Bermuda Breakthrough story will show you how to shift your beliefs about the fear of success. In that chapter I teach a strategic plan on how to identify and break free of the fear of success and the feelings of unworthiness.

For now, I want you to answer the question: Do you believe you can have it all?

Did you answer "yes," "no," or "it depends"? Now let me ask you the same question in a different way.

Do you believe you are worthy to have it all?

How did you respond to the question this time? That is the answer I am most interested in. This segment of *Don't Mess With the Princess!* is about you getting in touch with your desires...and shifting your beliefs about those desires.

Desires placed in your heart come from God, the very Source that will help you manifest the desires.

When you know without doubt you are worthy of having it all, you release the power of possibility. You become aware of the people and opportunity that will help you achieve your desires.

Please realize that the concept of "having it all" doesn't occur at one time in your life. Begin viewing your life in stages...

First you have the wonderful stage of education and discovering your career.

Then you may have the stage of marriage and family. You still maintain a healthy focus on yourself and your own development, but you may choose to work part-time or not at all to spend more time actively raising your children.

Just as you would never forget your grown children just because you are now a full-time business owner, you don't stop taking care of yourself or quit enjoying personal interests when you are a full-time mom.

The next stage in your life comes when your children are more independent. You might choose to focus on your career even more. You travel the world, exploring exotic cities, cultures, and people. Maybe you choose to volunteer more and are able to make a greater contribution outside your home and family life.

The point I am trying to make with the "You can have it all" concept is more about *creating a mindset that you are* **worthy** *of it all.*

And God, in His infinite love, wants you to enjoy this life you've been given—to savor every stage of it. The best gift you can give God is what you make of your life and how you glorify Him with the life He gave you.

You are meant to create miracles in your life, dear Princess. And you have everything you need to make your life exceptional! The only thing that will ever hold you back is you—and your beliefs.

Expect the Miraculous

I want to share with you a few of the miracles that have occurred in my life since shifting the belief that I am worthy of having it all.

Two years ago I realized I had the desire to enjoy a friendship with my former husband Mark. At first, I didn't really believe it could happen. I didn't have any examples of divorced people being friends. And my feeble belief created my reality. Mark was not open to "being friends." However, even a meager belief is powerful and can grow into a strong conviction. I continued to desire a friendship and held the space for it to happen. And over time our relationship began to evolve.

Today, we meet for coffee and share stories about our children and even who we're dating! When Mark comes to my house to pick up the kids, he comes in and hangs out for a while. Just last week he stopped by to show us his new car, and we all went for a cruise in it!

I would never have believed a divorced family could remain intact, supportive, and involved in each other's lives to the extent that we are.

We really can have it all...

I write these final chapters of *Don't Mess With the Princess!* overlooking the Caribbean Ocean. Like I said, I'm on a cruise by myself to finish the book. I have written chapters of this book all over the world—from Paris to Prague; from Munich to Maui; from Tahiti to Texas; and from thirty-five thousand feet above the earth on Delta Airlines to sea level on the Royal Caribbean Cruise Line!

Fourteen years ago, when I was stuck in fear, trapped in limiting beliefs, and ensnared in unworthiness issues, I never would have imagined—or dared to dream—that I would be living such an adventurous and miraculous life!

Let my life be your example that you really can have it all. And what it takes to have it all is the belief that you can.

You were born to be blessed to be a blessing to others!

So what about you?

Where do you need to shift your beliefs about having it all? About being worthy? Write what is resonating within you...

_____

_____

_____

_____

_____

_____

_____

_____

List some of the areas of your life that you want to develop and grow. Believe that you are worthy to have your goals and desires.

_____

_____

_____

_____

Anything is possible, Princess! My hope for you is you adopt the belief that you are worthy to "have it all." You were born to be blessed and to be a rich blessing for others.

Big Lie #4: It Has to Be Perfect

The Perfection Syndrome has kept women small and stuck for far too long. We use the excuse "It has to be perfect" to keep us from building a business, writing a book, hosting a dinner party, or even volunteering in our community.

Where did we learn we had to be perfect to be accepted, successful, and loved? It is one of the greatest lies society teaches us. Nevertheless, the real culprit here is not society, but you and your willingness to let that belief stop you.

The bottom line is most women fall captive to the Perfection Syndrome because it gives them a way out of really trying. If they step up and gave their goal a try they would have to deal with their greater fear...

What do you think is a woman's greatest fear when it comes to trying new things?

I'd like to reveal the answer to you by asking a question...

What do you think most women are truly committed to?

Is their greatest commitment helping other people? Supporting a cause, a ministry, or a charity? Building a big business? Finding cures for diseases?

Nope, sadly it's none of these...

If you are like most women, your greatest commitment is...

Looking Good!

Our culture is so driven by looking good and avoiding pain that it's normal for us to be affected by this driving force. Most women are so afraid of messing up, looking dumb, making a mistake, possibly failing, and... not looking good!

Until we deny our deep-seated need to "look good," we continue to hold ourselves back.

Let your commitment to "making an impact" or "achieving your dreams" be greater than your commitment to "looking good" and "avoiding pain."

If we were truly committed to feeding the homeless instead of looking good or avoiding pain, we would be relentlessly raising money. If we were more committed to tithing than to looking good or avoiding pain, we would be excited about building our businesses to million-dollar, even billion-dollar status. If we were more committed to being an encourager than to looking good or avoiding pain, we would send that card, make that phone call, and deliver that meal.

Think back in your own life and identify the times you stopped yourself from going all out because you didn't want to take the chance of making a mistake or looking like you "don't have it all together."

Write down one of those occasions here:

_____

_____

_____

_____

_____

_____

What could have occurred if you were willing to shift your commitment to "look good" and be willing to mess up, look stupid, get dirty, and practice something until you do it well.

I can remember when I first began building my direct sales business. I wouldn't give opportunity meetings because I didn't think I knew the marketing plan perfectly. I didn't want to make a mistake or look stupid in my presentation.

My sponsor shared with me how she went through the same thing but realized that she actually created more of a connection with her prospects when she made some mistakes and wasn't so perfect.

"Imagine that!" I thought to myself.

The next week I had nine prospects at my first opportunity meeting. I was so nervous! And I looked it. But that didn't matter at all, and I completely forgot about "not looking good" when three of the nine people signed up with my company.

Today, I give really good opportunity meetings. I mean, they are smokin'! But before I gave smokin' presentations, I gave pretty good ones. And before I gave pretty good presentations, I gave okay ones. And before I gave okay presentations, I gave horrible ones!

Tom Watson Sr. of IBM once hired a man to take care of the company's investment portfolio. On one occasion, this man lost the company millions of dollars. When the unlucky employee approached the CEO to give his resiqnation, Mr. Watson looked at him and said, "You just cost this company millions of dollars educating you. You're the last person leaving this company!" This corporate giant gives us another example of releasing your commitment to looking good and avoiding pain or failure. Change your belief of failure to:

"Anything worth doing is worth failing-forward at, until I get it right."

Are you willing to overcome your need for "looking good" and "avoiding pain" in order to build your business? Enjoy a delicious relationship? Learn a language?

Make a list of the areas in your business and personal life that your Perfection Syndrome has stopped you from wildly stepping out and growing:

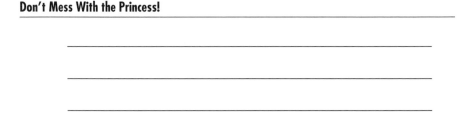

Let go of the lie that "It has to be perfect." Start reaching for goals that cause you to break through your need to look good, and you will begin living life powerfully and living a life you love!

Big Lie #5: It's a Man's World

If I were going to write a male-bashing segment, this would be the perfect place to put it. But that is not the approach a Princess would take. And, frankly, that type of outdated thinking would be out of sync with the transformation happening in the world today. No, I prefer to take a different approach to eliminate this lie—and that is by simply telling the truth...

The truth about our world is this: It's not a man's world. It's not a woman's world. It's a human being world. To go even deeper in this thought, we are human beings having a spiritual experience. And standing upon that reality...

We are one.

So how do we work together to heal and transform our planet in unity? I believe we begin by realizing we are one and then celebrating the uniqueness that we each offer to each other.

What Women Can Learn From Men

I stated earlier in Chapter Two that I believe women are wired with particular strengths and have innate abilities. Now let's address the innate gifts that men possess from which we can gain value. Women can learn a lot from men on how to handle rejection, self-esteem, success, and failure.

Men Are Wired to Externalize Their Problems

Picture this...

A man and a woman go to the department store to buy a pair of jeans. They both find their size and proceed to the fitting rooms. Let's peak in the two different dressing rooms and see what's going on...

The woman tries on the pair of jeans and realizes they are too tight. She can't even zip them up. She looks at herself in the mirror and thinks, "I'm getting fat. I've got to lose some weight."

The man in his own dressing room also notices his jeans are too tight. He looks at the tag in the jeans to check out the size and he thinks, "Hmmm. They must have put the wrong size on these jeans."

Hah! Isn't that true? Men tend to blame an outside source while women tend to blame themselves. Men are wired to externalize the problem.

We women can learn something from how men externalize problems. The next time you're faced with a negative situation—a disgruntled boss, a disappointed husband, rude behavior by a friend—don't internalize and emotionalize these circumstances. Simply notice them for what they are: a reflection of what's going on in that person's life. Consider the possibility that it has nothing to do with you.

I remember the first day of one particular Rich Life Mastermind Retreat. I had a new client participating who I knew had great expectations of the program. When the participants took turns sharing their business ideas, he began fidgeting in his seat. Immediately I internalized his behavior and began thinking that he didn't like the program.

Finally, after several people had shared their entrepreneurial venture, he looked at me sternly and whispered, "I need to talk to you on the break."

Again I internalized his behavior and even imagined him quitting the coaching program! I couldn't see at the time how ridiculous it was to jump to that assumption.

At the break he rushed over to me, grabbed my arm, and said, "I am blown away by how powerful this program is!" I stared at him for a moment, caught in my confusion at what I thought was going on, only to find out I had it all wrong. I doubt he noticed, for he hurried on. "Being around these kinds of people has shown me that I've been thinking way too small!"

Are you in the habit of internalizing people's behaviors and their life's problems? Take a cue from how men are wired and try externalizing the situation. Consider the possibility that the circumstance or negative behavior has nothing to do with you.

Men Are Taught in Childhood About Law of Averages and How to Deal With Failures

Most little boys were taken outside as a toddler and taught how to hit a baseball. From an early age, their dad or uncle or big brother would hand them a bat and say, "You're going to swing this bat to hit this ball. You'll miss the ball more times than you'll hit the ball. But that's okay. Just keep swinging."

Then, the little boy would swing...and swing...and swing. He would swing dozens of time and never even hit the ball. This didn't trouble him because he was told that to miss the ball was "normal." Then, after 217 swings, the bat would finally meet the ball. The little boy would feel so excited and have so much pride in himself, he would conclude that the having 217 "failures" was worth it just because that one single hit felt so good!

But most little girls aren't given this same, safe proving ground. They are never taught how to deal with failure. They were not encouraged by adults to accept failure in the pursuit of excellence—in other words, to be willing to miss the ball or to hear "No" a thousand times and not take it personally. They have never been taught that they must deal with failure if they want to experience success.

Women must retrain their thinking when it comes to failure and rejection. When you can change your belief about failure and see it as a stepping stone to success, you'll begin to celebrate the no's and realize they are getting you that much closer to a yes! Train your mind, like a little boy playing baseball, and accept the Law of Averages, getting a no, and dealing with rejection as the "normal" process to achieving success.

Men Rely on Discernment to Make Commitments

Society labels men as being commitment-phobic. I disagree. The men I interviewed for this book as well as the male friends I have in my life have a tremendous ability to commit. However, the process they use for deciding whether to choose commitment is very different than that of most women.

Think of it this way: When a woman meets a new friend she uses her intuition to know right away if she wants to spend time with that person. She makes the choice relatively fast. We see this behavior exaggerated in female teenagers where they meet a new person, have an intuition about whether the person can be trusted, and jump into a friendship.

"Do you want to be my friend?" is almost always answered with "Sure!" Females are quick to commit to friendships, activities, and relationships.

Men are different! They rely more on facts, statistics, and proof before they can make a decision to commit. This takes time.

I encourage you to change your perception about men and their "inability to commit" and see them as people who make commitment decisions with discernment. And discernment, unlike intuition, is not instantaneous. They need a lot more time to make their decision. But when they do, they commit full out.

Men Are Solution-Oriented in Problem Solving

For most women, the primary goal when faced with a problem is to "feel better." Their judgment of whether or not the problem is solved is based upon how they feel.

Men's primary goal in facing a problem is to solve it. They can even deal with the reality that solving the problem sometimes leads to feeling bad. While they have a strong desire to look good, they refrain from connecting the looking good with feeling good.

While you don't want to become like a man in this realm, you can learn an important lesson from their problem-solving ability: Be okay with the possibility that, in problem solving, you may cause someone to get angry with you. Occasionally you will have to give up your desire to "feel good" and "look good" to successfully solve inevitable problems. I talk about this extensively in Big Lie #4 of this chapter.

What I desire to have happen in this segment of the book is for you to realize that men are not your enemy. They are not holding you back. Change your beliefs about men and the value they bring to your life and you will begin attracting men who will support and encourage you to be your best.

Focus on men's strengths. Visualize unity with the sexes. Acknowledge the men in your life who support and encourage you, and you will attract more of the same.

The next step to destroy the belief that it's a man's world is to look at the facts...

Here are the most recent facts about business in our world. According to *The Center for Women's Business Research*:

- Over 80 percent of marketing efforts are geared toward women. Retailers know that it is women who are buying the furniture, clothes, vacations, cars, and houses. Women hold the purse strings of our world!
- One in every eighteen adult women in the United States is a business owner.
- Women-owned businesses employ one out of seven working Americans.
- Over three-fourths of network marketers are women.

So the questions need to be asked...

Why is it that so few women plan to be millionaires or billionaires? Why is it not the woman's responsibility, as much as the man's, to reach for the top?

Is it because we've been programmed from birth, from our fairy tales, novels, magazines, and television shows to believe that catching the man means catching the cash?

Women have got to quit relying on men to be their financial support. A man is not your financial plan! You are.

Okay, savvy Princess...it is time for you to claim your power in business and in life. It is your turn to step up, declare what you want, and believe that what you do makes a difference!

What is resonating with you right now?

_____

_____

_____

_____

What do you want to create with your life?

_____

_____

_____

_____

Whom do you need to ask for assistance?

_____

_____

_____

_____

What is your next step in achieving this?

_____

_____

_____

_____

You have the power to transform these lies. And you're doing it! I am so proud of the powerful woman you are. Now I want you to find a comfortable place to kick back and relax, because in the next chapter we're going to talk about sex, dating, love, and the Princess!

"Life loves to be taken by the lapel and told, 'I'm with you kid. Let's go!'"

—Maya Angelou

Chapter 8

Sex. Dating. Love. And the Princess

Deep in every woman's heart is a longing for a man who loves, cherishes, and adores her. She has a deep-seated desire to be pursued, prized, treasured, and made love to by someone who is devoted to her forever.

Most women have become numb to this innate desire. Their relationship experience has left them hurt, empty, and resigned. And this leads them to believe that a healthy and loving relationship doesn't exist for them. Or, even worse, they convince themselves that they really don't care about "that stuff" anyway. They allow their career, children, pet, or one-night stands to fill their innate desire for an intimate relationship with their Soul Mate.

Are you denying your innate desire for real love?

Nothing on the planet is more fundamentally your birthright than your feminine sexuality being expressed and celebrated in the safety of a warm, loving, and supportive relationship. The beauty you bring just by being a female is phenomenal. And you deserve a man who loves, cherishes, and adores you, just because you are you!

I want to make a note before we get into this segment that this chapter is for the woman who wants a long-term marital relationship. If you are at a place in your life where you want to explore different men and a variety of relationships, let yourself! Allow for this time in your life without self-judgment. Don't deny it or pretend you want exclusivity, because you think it "looks good" or that's what people say is best for you. When you allow yourself to be fully self-expressed in what you really want, you are living a life of integrity. And integrity creates the space for you to evolve into an exclusive relationship naturally.

One year after my divorce I began to date. Coming out of an eighteen-year marriage, I had the mindset that every man I dated was "supposed" to become exclusive. This was torture! I put so much unnecessary pressure on myself. When I made the decision to just enjoy dating—void of any commitment—I gave myself the much needed space to just explore... myself!

Having said that, please know that this chapter is for the Princess who is ready to be in an exclusive relationship that leads to marriage and wants to learn how to attract it.

Are you ready?

Let's begin with talking about what doesn't work.

Society's Dating Dance

Let's be real here... The way "society" approaches dating doesn't work and following it will not lead to a healthy, fulfilling relationship.

The core fundamentals of building a relationship according to society is:

> You meet.
>
> You date.
>
> You have sex.
>
> Then you live together, get married, or break up.

Have you been seduced into believing in society's system for love? Do you believe that the path to finding your soul mate includes giving yourself sexually with no expectation of a future? Do you view jumping in the sack by the third or fourth date as normal or expected?

144

There is a better way to samba through the Dance of Dating. It begins with you declaring what you really want. If you are a Princess, then you want a man who is willing to pursue you, take his time in getting to know you, and, most importantly, is willing to step up and be the man deserving of you!

Do you realize the power you bring to a relationship just by being female?

The Power of Your Feminine Sexuality

Remember the movie *Anna and the King*, which told the story of a widowed schoolteacher who travels with her son to Asia to teach the children of the king of Siam? Polygamy is the common practice of the monarchy, so the king has a number of concubines and wives.

The king makes the mistake of falling in love with the schoolteacher. He becomes angry with himself, for he has upset the order of his own kingdom. *He is accustomed to having the affection of women who serve him. But he has never had a relationship with a woman—until he met Anna.*

This represents the "reality" of most men today. They are used to having women "serve them" sexually. In any direction you turn, women feel not just the opportunity, but the pressure to be sexually active. Think of the dozens of magazine covers boasting articles that will give women the latest tip on how to "do" a man—as though it is a woman's job to provide the best sexual experience possible.

The desire to be pursued and courted, to have sex with someone you love as opposed to someone you barely know, to be certain of a man's affection and loyalty—these are deep female cravings that did not vanish with the sexual revolution. Don't fall for society's message!

Picture the scene from the movie *Anna and the King* where the two of them are dancing outside his palace on a veranda looking out over the ocean. The king utters a line that could be echoed by men throughout the ages. He says, "I didn't know there was so much to be had in the love of one woman."

That's the secret that you possess, Sweet Princess. You are capable of inviting a man into a relationship so deep and valuable that *it is worth the reordering of his entire life.*

Remember this: Men become men by doing battle with their fears. When a man pursues a woman and learns how to love, cherish, and adore her, he is well into the process of becoming the man God has in mind for him to be.

A teenage boy must walk across the dance floor to ask a girl to dance. He has to pick up the phone to ask for a date and deal with rejection. Then, when he begins to date a girl, if that girl refrains from engaging in the sexual experience right away, he will have the opportunity to win her over with his mind, his creativity, his wit, his charm, and his ability to be more than a "boy with hormones." He will evolve into a man who has control over his sexuality.

In his book, *Wild at Heart*, John Eldredge, says:

> Sexual favor before marriage simply stunts the growth of boys into real men. When men can move outside the narrow confines of their own immediate needs, battle their sexuality and ride it like a wild stallion until its power is harnessed and under control, then he gets the great gift of being able to use his sexuality for a larger purpose.

The bottom line is this: Sex is all-consuming! It's designed that way. Give yourself and your new relationship time to evolve together before you become sexual. Give yourself the opportunity to discern whether this man is what you really want before you move into sexual expression together.

If you ever feel guilty that you are denying sexual favor to your man—as though it is just too hard on him to expect that kind of restraint—know this: While you may have a fear that he'll turn elsewhere for the sex, this guilt and fear reveals how little you understand about the way men come to be real men—and the vital role you play in that process.

The men I interviewed for this book admitted they will follow a woman's lead where sex is concerned. And, if they really like the woman, they secretly hope she wants to hold off on creating a sexual relationship! They know how sex can change everything. They know that sex in dating looks a lot like love but isn't love at all.

Dating and courting a woman is an ancient rite of passage that helps turn a boy into a man you can depend on, expect something of, and trust with your life.

Don't settle for anything less!

Julia Roberts in *Pretty Woman* didn't settle. Remember the scene where Richard Gere makes Julia Roberts an offer he thought she couldn't resist? He promises to put her up in a swanky condo, give her access to his credit cards, and be his on-call girlfriend. And she declines! Hah! The prostitute has a higher standard for herself than many other women. She sees herself as a woman, deserving of the love and commitment of a man. She knows what she has to offer. She has realized her beauty, telling Gere, "I want more."

I wonder how many of us long to say those words to a man. How many of you long for a man who sees in you a love he cannot live without? A man who wants to commit his life to you, not just his body or his free time?

Sexual power is right at the heart of who you are as a woman. It is power that is rightfully yours. When sex is an investment you make in the love of your life, it multiplies into the most intimate and pleasurable relationship you ever dreamed of. It blesses every other part of your life with your man.

Believe That Real Love Exists

You can't manifest something you don't believe in. Recommit to the belief that Real Love does exist. And never settle for anything less than this.

You are meant to be loved and valued, cherished and supported by a man whose face lights up when he sees you.

How can you shift your belief that men can and will love you? Even if you've been hurt before, you can create the belief that real love exists. Real love moves through hardship, difficulty, or pain. That's just part of being human. It's what we call "life!" There is a man who is willing to go through life with you. Do you really believe that?

Until you shift that belief, you won't be able to see the loving qualities a man gives you. Do you really get that? If your belief is, "Men are assholes," then that is the type of man you will attract. You will always attract whatever supports your belief. Do you see how important it is to shift your internal belief about men and their ability to love, support, and cherish women?

One way to shift the belief is to find couples who replicate what you want in marriage. Who is enjoying the type of relationship you desire? Hang out with them. Study them. Ask them questions. Just be around them. This will give you a quantum leap in shifting your beliefs and creating a mind set of "Real Love Exists!"

Another way to adopt empowering beliefs about attracting real love is with mantras.

One of my mantras about love is: *"I am in love with a man who adores me!"* I repeat this mantra throughout the day. It has made a profound difference in how I notice love. There is love all around me! Where I was once blind to acts of love, I now see them all over my world. That's powerful!

Do you really want to shift your belief about men and how loving they can be—especially to you?! Write your mantras about love and declare them everyday.

Write your Mantra here:

_____

_____

_____

_____

Attracting Real Love

The next vital step is choosing what you want and declaring it. If you want exclusivity, say it. If your desire is marriage, declare it. Be a woman who is true to her desires. It doesn't make you sound needy or weak. The weak woman is the one who doesn't have the courage to state what she really wants and then pretends she is happy and fulfilled with less than her wonderful, true, core desires.

If you're already in an exclusive relationship, this exercise will help you shift your beliefs about your man. You will actually begin noticing wonderful traits about your husband or boyfriend that you were blind to.

So, what do you want?

What do you want in an intimate relationship? Write your desire here:

_____

_____

_____

_____

Congratulations! You are a bold and courageous woman!

Now, I'd like for you to be specific in defining your Soul Mate. Make a list of attributes, character qualities, physical traits—everything that describes your Dream Guy. Have fun with this. Get as specific as possible: If you could have everything you want in your man, what would it be? Write down those attributes:

Spiritual Qualities:

_____

_____

_____

_____

Character Traits:

_____

_____

_____

_____

Physical Description:

_____

_____

_____

_____

Personality:

_____

_____

_____

_____

Family Goals and Desires:

_____

_____

_____

_____

Occupation:

_____

_____

_____

_____

Hobbies:

_____

_____

_____

_____

Financial:

_____

_____

_____

_____

Location (where he lives):

_____

_____

_____

_____

Mindset:

_____

_____

_____

_____

Other:

_____

_____

_____

_____

Wow! Isn't that fun? That exercise will help you gain clarity. Clarity is power. Knowing what you want is the quantum leap you take to manifest that power. Your choice, your desires have just been declared to the world!

Be the Person You Are Looking to Attract

Okay, so I played a little trick on you. While identifying what you want in your Dream Guy is vital; the more important point here is for you to look over that list and BE THAT PERSON you want to attract! This is crucial for your manifestation process. We'll be going into this powerful process in my next book.

So, you have some work to do Princess! You are the manifestation of Real Love. Be that woman of character. Be that personality. Adopt those empowering beliefs. Be the spiritual leader you're looking for in a man. Be the financial rock you want in your Soul Mate. Become everything you want...and that, my dear Princess, is the most powerful practice to manifesting your Dream Man and the most delicious, extraordinary relationship in existence.

You will manifest a relationship (or improve the one you have) to be one they write movies about!

"One can never consent to creep when one feels an impulse to soar."

—Helen Keller

Epilogue

I share with you a note that I just received from a young woman who was raised by a mother who never claimed her feminine power. This 25 year old daughter writes...

"No one knows about how I go to bed every night and begin to think.... why me? Am I not good enough? Am I gonna end up alone like my mom?..."

Now that you've read *Don't Mess With the Princess!* I hope you realize that when you play small, think little of yourself or what's possible for you, settle for less, or try to "be nice to fit in", you are not helping the planet! And your children, your community and your world needs you to think big, act big and be big.

I want you to claim your power—and that power is your femininity!

Whether it's in business, your family, or your community, my desire for you is that you accept this power in humility and then go out and kick some ass! What you do matters. You have a vital role in this world and that role is the successful, self-expressed, happy and fulfilled woman that you are.

My thirteen year old son, Connor was asked to write a paper about a person he respects and looks up to. I was humbled to read what he wrote about me...

"You teach me a lot about life by living it. You love God more than anything and you show me that I can have it all. I am blessed to have a mother like you."

When you know what you know... what you know... and what you know is that you are beautiful, feminine, fierce, demure, daring, loving, and lovable; and what you do in life matters... when you know that, then you will be the Princess this world so desperately needs you to be. Please, step up to the calling you've now been given. Powerfully choose everyday who you want to be and then be that woman! You get to choose today and every day. Play big. Have fun. And live full out!

Richest blessings to you Powerful Princess,

LISA!

Lisa Jimenez M.Ed.
Kona, Hawaii
www.Rx-Success.com
(954) 755-3670

Learning Resources by Lisa Jimenez

172 pages, hard-cover book

Conquer Fear! Ending Procrastination and Self-Sabotage to Achieve What You Really Want

Why is it that two people can take the same goal-setting class, and one will achieve their goals, while the other will allow fear, lack of focus, procrastination and self-sabotage to destroy their efforts, and never accomplish the very thing they say they want? That very question, and experiencing it countless times with the sales force I was leading in a direct selling company, led me to write this book, *Conquer Fear*.

Most books written on this subject only cover the psychology factor of fear, which doesn't create lifelong change. There's something deeper. The other factor that, Conquer Fear answers is an issue of the heart. The way to conquer fear and create courage is to cultivate faith. The opposite of fear is faith. It is faith that fosters courage, boldness and conviction. It is only through faith that we can banish fear, anxiety, procrastination, and all the other symptoms that fear creates. The missing link was that most people don't cultivate their faith. They have negative belief barriers that limit their success. The startling truth is, "The only person keeping you from achieving your goals is you."

Change your beliefs—and you change your behaviors.

Change your behaviors—and you change your results.

It was when we began living our life by this statement that we began to see incredible success:

Conquer Fear, through the blending of the two disciplines of psychology and theology, is your tool to changing your results through first changing your beliefs. Through this book, you will discover the core truths about goal-setting, maintaining focus, motivation, and creating momentum. You will uncover the reasons behind why you do what you do. You will uncover the hidden needs and beliefs behind your behavior, and cultivate your faith so you have the courage to change them.

Whether you are an entrepreneur, a director of a company or a parent, Conquer Fear will empower you to break through procrastination. self-limiting beliefs, and cultivate your courage to accomplish all you're meant to achieve. —L. J.

172 pages, hard-cover book   **Order #B2, $27**

Radical Recruiting! on 6 Audio CDs & Workbook

Lisa Jiménez, M.Ed.

Learn how to attract and recruit the winners! This audio album should be in every Network Marketer's library. In it, you will learn how to change your mindset and shatter your fear of recruiting. You'll master the 5-step sponsoring process and learn how to create an easy to use follow-up system. You'll learn the secrets to crafting a powerful presentation and one-on-one talk. You have all you need to build the organization you've always dreamed of. Learn how to use it to your ultimate advantage with this powerful six audio CD album and workbook.

Radical Recruiting will help you build your organization fast. You will learn an easy to duplicate 5-step recruiting process that will help you:

- Discover and eliminate your hidden fears about prospecting;
- Find out where to find the best prospects;
- Learn how to make powerful presentations to build your image—and your confidence;
- Practice the best strategy for successful follow-up;
- Discover the secrets to overcome the toughest objections;
- Learn the most effective close to help your prospect say yes; and
- Create momentum to make building your business more fun.

If you're serious about enrolling more leaders, making more money, and having more fun prospecting, then Radical Recruiting can show you the way. In this program, Lisa Jimenez M.Ed., digs deep to the root of prospecting to show you how to take your business to the next level. Lisa will empower you with the personal growth tools and dynamite prospecting skills you need to boost your business now! She uses her real-world experience of building a big business herself, to show you how to attract and retain the winners. Lisa's 5-step recruiting process is motivating to follow and gets results.

6 audio CDs and 32-page workbook **Order #A5, $127**

27 Tips to Radical Recruiting! E-Coaching Program

27 Tips delivered via email in your inbox each day for 27 days to motivate and inspire your radical recruiting efforts! These are the personal growth tools and dynamite prospecting skills you need to boost your business now!

Picture this... every morning, first thing when you get up, you open your e-mail and I'm in your inbox. I'm there with one specific thing you can do that day to grow your business just a little bit more. The next day, another e-mail bell—it's another message from me with another tip to help you find yet one more leader for your organization. Day three another bell... Day four another bell...

For the next 27 days you and I are going to be connected in a journey of challenge, adventure and growth. These recruiting tips will take you to the upper reaches of your company's compensation plan!

$27

27 Tips to Conquering Your Fear! E-Coaching

Online Coaching Program. 27 Tips delivered via email in your inbox each day for 27 days to help you Conquer Your Fears and Achieve Your Dreams!

$27

Here's How To Order

Our staff is ready to answer your questions and assist you with your mail or phone order. Please use this order form to organize your phone order before you call our toll-free number. Order online www.Rx-Success.com.

Your Name _____

MLM Co. _____

Address _____

City _____ State _____ Zip _____

Office Phone _____ Home Phone _____

Fax _____

PHONE: 1-800-489-7391 or (954) 755-3670

MAIL: **Rx Success, Inc.**
4630 N. University Dr. Suite #449
Coral Springs, FL 33067

Method of Payment:

____ Check or Money Order payable to Rx Success, Inc.
No cash or CODs please.

____ Visa ____ M/C ____ Amex ____ Diners ____ Discover
Card Number _____

Expiration _____ Signature _____

For shipments to an address other than your own, fill in below:

Your Name _____

Address _____

City _____ State _____ Zip _____

Phone _____

Gift Card To _____

From _____

90-day, 100% money back guarantee on
items returned in resalable condition.